DATE DUE

~~MY 12 '9~~			
NO 17 '00			
~~DE 4 '00~~			
~~FE 8 '03~~			
~~FE 12 '03~~			

THE
NIXON
MEMO

THE

NIXON

MEMO

Political Respectability, Russia, and the Press

MARVIN KALB

The University of Chicago Press   Chicago & London

Marvin Kalb,
the Edward R. Murrow Professor of Press and Public Policy, is
director of the Joan Shorenstein Barone Center on the Press, Politics and
Public Policy at Harvard's Kennedy School of Government. Before joining
Harvard in 1987, he was one of television's premier journalists, the chief
diplomatic correspondent for CBS and then NBC. He has authored
or co-authored eight other books.

The University of Chicago Press, Chicago 60637
The University of Chicago Press, Ltd., London
© 1994 by The University of Chicago
All rights reserved. Published 1994
Printed in the United States of America
03 02 01 00 99 98 97 96 95 94   1 2 3 4 5
ISBN: 0-226-42299-2 (cloth)

Library of Congress Cataloging-in Publication Data

Kalb, Marvin L.
    The Nixon memo : Political respectability, Russia, and the press / Marvin
Kalb.
    p.   cm.
    Includes bibliographical references (p.) and index.
    1. Nixon, Richard M. (Richard Milhous), 1913–1994—Views on Russia.
2. Press and politics—United States.   3. United States—Foreign
relations—Russia.   4. Russia—Foreign relations—United States.
5. Presidents—United States—Election—1992.   I. Title.
E856.K345   1994
973.924′092—dc20   94–27206
                                                                        CIP

In memory of

ROSE BELL GREEN

who taught me to revere prose and

to be skeptical of politicians

CONTENTS

Acknowledgments

ix

ACKNOWLEDGMENTS

First, I wish to express my thanks to all of my colleagues at Harvard's Kennedy School of Government for their encouragement. For the past seven years, the Joan Shorenstein Barone Center on the Press, Politics and Public Policy, which I have had the pleasure of directing, has been an exciting place for research and writing in the emerging field of press/politics.

Nancy Palmer, the assistant director of the Center, helped in a thousand different ways, anticipating and solving problems, controlling the flow of papers and students, and serving on many occasions as a sounding board for ideas. Frederick Schauer, the Frank Stanton Professor of the First Amendment, read the manuscript with his usual diligence and offered invaluable suggestions, big and small. I extend my gratitude, too, to Michele Johnson for her mastery of the new computer age, her dedication as a researcher, and her cooperative spirit; to Russell Stevens for his research assistance in the early stage of the book's preparation; and to Susan Burns for her assistance in the final stage.

I have worked with three deans of the Kennedy School. Graham Allison, Robert Putnam, and Albert Carnesale have helped to create an atmosphere of academic excellence and excitement about public policy that has encouraged members of the faculty to pursue new paths of discovery and, while double-checking old assumptions, to explore new ones, with a view toward understanding and then trying to solve the problems of modern-day governance. They, too, have my thanks.

I am also grateful to dozens of journalists and government officials, past and present, who talked to me on the record or on background. Dimitri Simes of the Carnegie Endowment for International Peace and William Safire of the *New York Times* were especially helpful.

My friend Morton Janklow was patient and helpful. His many contributions to me—and to so many other writers—should themselves be the stuff of books. He is a pioneer in the field.

After consultation with two of my colleagues here, Pippa Norris and Marion Just, I sent the manuscript to John Tryneski, senior editor at the University of Chicago Press. Tryneski responded with enthusiasm. Consistent with a university press tradition, Tryneski sent the manuscript to a number of outside readers, who wrote long, gracious, thoughtful critiques. Though to this day I do not know their identities, I valued their contributions and incorporated many of their suggestions into the manuscript. Thank you, whoever you are. I valued, too, the professional assistance of Rina Ranalli, Jennie Lightner, and other members of the staff at the University of Chicago Press.

I also wish to express my gratitude to William P. Green, Bernard Kalb, and Harry Schwartz for their editorial suggestions.

Finally, my wife, Madeleine Green Kalb, a writer and scholar, took time from her own busy schedule to edit *The Nixon Memo* with her characteristic dedication to style, clarity, and accuracy. She has provided encouragement and support throughout the project. She is a wonder, and as always I am in her debt.

The fault is mine, and mine alone, for any misdiagnosis or misplaced comma.

Cambridge, Massachusetts
June 1994

1

THE IDEA

On March 10, 1992, Super Tuesday in the presidential primary calendar, a most extraordinary story appeared on the front page of the *New York Times*. The headline caught my attention: "Nixon Scoffs at Level of Support for Russian Democracy by Bush." The lead of the story, written by Thomas Friedman, then the paper's diplomatic correspondent, was equally dramatic. "Former President Richard M. Nixon has sharply criticized President Bush and Secretary of State James A. Baker 3d for what he calls the Administration's pathetic support of the democratic revolution in Russia. He says one of the historic opportunities of this century is being missed." According to Friedman, these views were contained in a memo that Nixon wrote and circulated to a limited number of officials and journalists. There was no doubt Friedman had seen the memo.

The *Times* quoted the Nixon memo as saying: "While the candidates have addressed scores of significant issues in the presidential campaign, the most important issue since the end of World War II—the fate of the political and economic reforms in Russia— has been virtually ignored." Nixon dismissed Western efforts to help Russia as "penny ante" and warned that if Boris Yeltsin and the emerging "democracy" in Russia collapsed, "we can kiss the peace dividend good-bye."

Then, reported the *Times*, Nixon laid a challenge before the

White House and a grim political forecast before the nation. "The mark of great political leadership is not simply to support what is popular," he wrote, "but to make what is unpopular popular if that serves America's national interest. In addition, what seems politically profitable in the short term may prove costly in the long term. The hot button issue in the 1950's was, 'Who lost China?' If Yeltsin goes down, the question of 'Who lost Russia?' will be an infinitely more devastating issue in the 1990's."

Why would Nixon raise such an inflammatory question at this time? Why would he attack Bush? Why on an issue of foreign policy, which was reputedly Bush's strong suit? Why during a particularly vulnerable time in Bush's reelection campaign?

These were instantly intriguing questions for anyone interested in presidential politics. I was at the time looking for a theme for a keynote speech that I was to deliver at the fifth anniversary celebration of the Joan Shorenstein Barone Center on the Press, Politics and Public Policy at Harvard's Kennedy School of Government. Nixon, as president, had done much to complicate my life. In the early 1970s, when I was chief diplomatic correspondent for CBS News in Washington, he wiretapped my home phone and put me on his "enemies list." (For more details, see Epilogue.) But now, as a controversial former president still intent on influencing his country's foreign policy, he unwittingly came to my assistance. The moment I saw his criticism of President Bush in the *New York Times,* I knew that I had found the theme for my speech.

Here were two prominent Republican politicians trapped in a major policy dispute on the front page of the world's most influential newspaper: one a disgraced ex-president forced to resign one step ahead of almost certain impeachment by the House of Representatives in the summer of 1974; the other an incumbent president suddenly confronted, in the midst of a contentious campaign, with stinging criticism from a most unlikely source. Here was a political drama in which the *Times* seemed to be playing a crucially central role. Here, too, was the tip of the iceberg on a story of global significance: after the dismantling of the Communist system in the old Soviet Union, what was America's responsibility for nurturing the fragile shoots of democracy and a free market economy in a new and revolutionary Russia?

   Within a few weeks, my initial research had produced some interesting information about Nixon, Bush, Clinton, Russia, Yeltsin, democratization, free market economic theories, the inner workings of the *New York Times,* the *Washington Post,* and *Time* magazine, press manipulation, and leaks—in other words, about the whole absorbing world of press/politics, which lies at the heart of our research at the Shorenstein Barone Center. The Nixon memo illustrated the intersection of press and politics: the artful maneuvering of an aging politician seeking political rehabilitation after the humiliation of the Watergate scandal; the reactions of the presidential candidates and congressional leaders; the mores and motivations of the competitive press; and the public policy that results from the collision or collaboration of the press with the politicians. These were the ingredients of the keynote address I delivered on April 24, 1992. My colleagues encouraged me to continue my research, which ultimately led to this book.

                              * * *

In the early 1990s the United States was at a turning point in its history. A deep recession was nibbling away at the national spirit, and, as the Cold War receded into history, Americans were thinking less about Russia and national security and more about domestic concerns and jobs. They were tired of politics-as-usual. They wanted change, but it was not clear how much change.

A year after reaching 89 percent in popularity polls following
the Persian Gulf War, President Bush was steadily losing ground.
Columnist Patrick Buchanan, with his isolationist rallying cry of
"America First," challenged him in the early primaries. A bruised
Governor Bill Clinton of Arkansas led the field of Democratic
contenders. Ross Perot, a Texas billionaire, emerged as an unpredictable deep-pockets candidate unattached to either party. Bush
heard the refrain for change but retained an aristocrat's confidence that his cause would ultimately prevail. His strategy seemed
to be taken from the handbook of a good football team seeking
back-to-back Super Bowl victories: play to your strengths, make
no mistakes, run the ball if possible, avoid turnovers.

Into this politically charged environment rode Richard Nixon,
one of the most divisive figures in recent American history. Questions rode along with him.

1. What prompted Nixon to write his memo attacking Bush?
   Why was someone traditionally associated with anti-
   Communism suddenly in the forefront of a pro-Russia foreign policy? Was his policy realistic? Was it in the national interest?
2. How did the Nixon memo leak? What was Nixon's role in
   the leak? How did Nixon use the press to advance his political agenda?
3. How did the press function during this Nixon operation?
   Were reporters setting the national agenda, or was Nixon?
   Were reporters aware of his attempts at manipulation? Were
   they capable of resisting them? What word best describes
   press behavior: competition, cooperation, collaboration,
   conspiracy?
4. What was the impact of the Nixon memo on public policy?

Did Nixon actually effect a change in U.S. policy toward Russia?

These questions, which emerged with the publication of the Nixon memo, ranged over the field of press/politics. More than ever before in U.S. history, the intersection of these two worlds has become the key to understanding the way in which government reaches decisions. This process, exciting at any other time, reaches feverish intensity during presidential campaigns. Nixon exploited this moment to try to secure his reputation as an elder statesman and to erase the stain of Watergate.

Nixon chose a foreign policy issue that flowed from his career-long interest in Russia and China—and gave it a new twist. A man with few fixed principles, shifting easily between pragmatism and party loyalty, he initially ran for office as an unflinching anti-Communist. He moved up the political ladder as a Red-baiter who accused President Harry Truman and Secretary of State Dean Acheson—the architects of the Cold War containment policy—of "treason" because they were "soft on Communism." As president, he pursued détente, arguing that survival in the nuclear age was more important than ideological consistency. Now he emerged as the number one salesman for Yeltsin and the new Russia.

This crusade was furthered by a sophisticated manipulation of the press. One of the first of the modern politicians to understand the true scope and power of the press, he always knew that reporters need news and conflict to survive in a competitive world. Nixon, who made news by simply stepping out on the stage, launched the most dramatic aspect of his strategy during the height of the primary season: he not only wrote a blistering memo critical of Bush's policy toward Russia and arranged for it to leak, but also organized a Washington conference for several hundred government officials, scholars, and journalists which served as an echo chamber for his views about Russian aid. The memo leaked the day before the conference opened.

Nixon assumed, like many other political observers, that Bush would win reelection, but he hedged his bets. He told an aide in Washington that he did not want to "deliver a rip-snorting attack on Clinton," which might have been expected of him, because "if . . . Clinton is elected, it would be very hard for me to reach out to him on the situation in Russia" (*New York Times,* April 28, 1994, p. A23). When Bush lost the election, Nixon instantly turned his attention to President-elect Bill Clinton, a Democrat who had demonstrated against the war in Vietnam that Nixon had waged.

It was clear from the beginning that Nixon would be my central character. He was different. Other politicians had come and gone, their time upon the stage defined by terms, appointments, or unforeseen events. There one day, gone the next—defeated, re-tired, or assassinated. Like Rasputin, Nixon had suffered a thou-sand forms of political death—dishonor, humiliation, and criti-cism—that would have destroyed any other politician. But not Nixon. For almost fifty years, from his first election to Congress in 1946 until his death in April 1994, he stubbornly refused to leave the stage. For generations of Americans, from the children of the Depression to the baby-boomers of the 1980s and 1990s, for those who were traumatized by the Kennedy assassination, divided by the Vietnam War, disillusioned by the Watergate scan-dal, and tranquilized by the Reagan administration, he was a per-manent presence—complex, troubling, a man Tom Wicker de-scribed as a "lonely introvert who rose to the top in the extroverted world of elective politics" (*New York Times,* April 24, 1994, section 4, p. E1).

What follows is not another biography of Nixon. It is, rather, the story of the Nixon memo as a vivid example of press/politics in action and of a shrewd and persistent politician's quest for renewed respectability.

2

"I'M ONE OF THE MOST HATED"

Understandably, Nixon's political life was divided into two parts: pre- and post-Watergate. In both parts, as he ascended to the presidency and then struggled to return from political oblivion, he developed a most unusual relationship with the press.

Nixon never liked reporters. He always felt the need to control, manage, taunt, tease, threaten, attack, and criticize the press. He often applied a surgeon's skill to the manipulation of newspaper publishers and television correspondents. At other times, he was about as delicate as an 800-pound gorilla. Yet, in an odd way, he respected the journalists' position in society, even if he did not fully understand it, and he recognized their importance to the political process and their value to him. Whenever he plotted a move, whether it was saving his spot on the GOP ticket in 1952 or agitating for aid to Russia in 1992, he found a prominent place for the press in his calculations.

As for the reporters, many of them (with a few notable exceptions, of course) never really liked Nixon, or felt particularly comfortable in his presence. Yet they knew a good story when they saw one, and throughout his career Nixon was always a good story.

In short, Nixon and the press established one of the strangest love-hate relationships in modern American history—using, misusing, and abusing each other with extraordinary frequency and little joy. Press and politics, politics and the press—they were an inseparable combination in the former president's career.

Early on, Nixon discovered the power of press manipulation for political ends. In 1952, when Dwight Eisenhower edged toward dumping the young and ambitious California senator from the vice-presidential spot on his ticket because of adverse reaction to the news that a group of conservative businessmen were supplementing the senator's salary with a $20,000 "slush fund," Nixon outmaneuvered the popular wartime hero by taking to the airwaves. He decided to defend his position in a nationwide television appearance. Although television was then in its infancy, Nixon grasped its latent capacity to advance his political agenda. He sat in an unadorned studio in Los Angeles. Looking into the lens of a single camera, he spoke of a dog named Checkers and his wife's Republican cloth coat; he spoke of his humble origins and his dedication to the Republican Party; and he appealed for popular support over the head of the party establishment. Among conservatives, Nixon became an overnight sensation. Among reporters, Nixon became an urgent story. Millions of calls and telegrams rained down on GOP headquarters, which suddenly found itself paralyzed by this massive outpouring of support.

Nixon's bold use of television catapulted him into the big leagues of American politics. "One must mark 1952 as the date that Richard Nixon discovered how spectacular the influence of television could be," wrote campaign chronicler Theodore H. White. "He reached for the first time nationally to stir the emotions of middle America and override the decisions of the party masters for his dismissal." Added scholar Garry Wills, "That broadcast saved Nixon's career, and made history" (Donovan and Scherer 1992, p. 40).

In dramatic fashion, Nixon was to learn in 1960 that television can boomerang. During his presidential campaign against Democratic Senator John F. Kennedy, the first in which television played a major role, Nixon had a choice. As vice-president, he could have decided to play it safe and refuse to debate his young challenger from Massachusetts, thereby denying Kennedy the national exposure and legitimacy that television provided. Though televised debates have become commonplace in recent campaigns, in 1960 the concept was new. Nixon, in a major miscalculation, overestimated his political strength and underestimated his opponent's ability to charm the lens. He bought the networks' proposal for four televised debates.

The first, on September 26, 1960, was memorable. Nixon was ill and foolishly refused makeup. Kennedy was suntanned, rested, and, by comparison, vigorous. Kennedy won the contest of appearances. Americans who only heard the debate on radio thought Nixon had won. An estimated 80 million Americans watched this opening debate, more than had watched any other event since Nixon's "Checkers" speech. Television proved its importance as one of the emerging arbiters of presidential politics.

For the first time in his meteoric career, Nixon had lost an election, and he was bitter. So, too, was his wife, Pat. One evening, shortly after the election, two reporters knocked on the door of Nixon's home in Washington. Nixon answered a few of their questions before Mrs. Nixon suddenly appeared and interrupted the informal exchange. "She was angry and, it was clear, not in control of her emotions. She damned the reporters and their colleagues for favoritism toward Kennedy that she said cost her husband the election" (Michael Kelly, *New York Times Magazine*, October 31, 1993, p. 64).

Nixon agreed with his wife. He believed that Kennedy had won with unfair help from the press. "The way the Kennedys played politics and the way the media let them get away with it left me angry and frustrated" (Kutler 1990, p. 49). The fault, he seemed to believe, did not lie with him, his strategy, or his policies, but with powerful politicians and reporters who were in an unrelenting conspiracy against him. Newspapers, he felt certain, were aligned against him, though the overwhelming majority were Republican in their editorial positions and ownership. He thought that television reporters were especially biased. They distorted his record. They favored his opponent. How could he possibly have won against such odds? He told one reporter that he would never again barnstorm the country, working airport fences "to press the flesh." What was the point?

In less than two years, Nixon was barnstorming California. His suspicions about press unfairness had hardened into a conviction, as time and again he felt that the press was out to get him, not to cover him objectively. In his race for governor, he got 47.5 percent of the approximately 6 million votes that had been cast, clearly not enough. At a concluding news conference, he showed an anti-press peevishness and resentment that were to become the hallmarks of his public persona. He felt sorry for himself: Nixon against the press, Nixon against his enemies. Even now, so many years later, his words deserve to be quoted and savored, for the underlying message was to recur in different settings and circumstances for the rest of his life.

"One last thing," he said, "I leave you gentlemen now, and you will now write it. You will interpret it. That's your right. But as I leave you, I want you to know—just think how much you are going to be missing. You won't have Nixon to kick around anymore, because, gentlemen, this is my last press conference, and it will be one in which I have welcomed the opportunity to test wits with you. I hope that what I have said today will at least make television, radio, the press . . . recognize that they have a right and a responsibility, if you're against a candidate, give him the shaft, but also recognize that if you give him the shaft, put one lonely reporter on the campaign who will report what the candidate said now and then." (Ambrose 1987, vol.1, p. 671. In an endnote, Ambrose writes: "There are a number of complete texts of the conference; there are some variations in them; I used the *New York Times* version of 11/8/62.")

Scholar Stanley I. Kutler wrote that as soon as the press conference ended, Nixon turned to H. R. ("Bob") Haldeman, then a young campaign aide, and said, "I finally told those bastards off, and every goddamned thing I said was true" (Kutler 1990, p. 55). When stories of the news conference ran the next morning, it was not his loss that was featured but, rather, his performance, his framing of the event, his attack on the press, his self-pity.

By the mid-1960s, Nixon, up from the mat, was again barnstorming, as he began his 1968 quest for the presidency. He moved to New York City, closer to the hub of the press, the *New York Times,* the television networks, Wall Street, the big barons of law and business. His thinking was logical. In 1960, he had lost an agonizingly close race. In 1964, he did not challenge Barry Goldwater, who ended up carrying the Republican standard to a devastating defeat. Who else but Nixon could now unite the conservative and liberal factions of the Republican Party? Who else but Nixon could win? But how? Nixon had not only a "plan" to end the divisive war in Vietnam (years later, he was to admit that he had no such "plan") but a new press strategy that was tough and dramatic. It depended on a new use of television to carry the candidate into the White House.

"What's on the tube is what counts," Nixon told his staff (Donovan and Scherer 1992, p. 41). He outlined the new, sophisticated side of American politics. Nowhere was it better described than in Joe McGinniss's 1969 book, *The Selling of the President,* which presented the repackaging of Nixon from "old" to "new" by a team of public relations and television specialists.

As William Gavin, a Nixon aide at the time, told the candidate in a memo, suggesting the nature of the sales pitch: "Voters are basically lazy, basically uninterested in making an effort to understand what they're talking about. . . . We've got to appear larger than life, and this is one great advantage of a film: it can be projected larger than life. We cannot win the election of 1968 with the techniques of 1952. We're not only in a television age . . . it's one of unease, of discontent, of frustration, largely undirected or multidirectional, diffuse" (McGinniss 1969, pp. 210–11).

In a November 28, 1967, memo by speechwriter Ray Price, one key element of the new revolutionary strategy was outlined. Because of television, Price wrote, what was now important was not objective reality but "the image of the candidate." He explained: "*We have to be very clear on this point: that the response* [of the voting public] *is to the image, not to the man,* since 99% of the voters have no contact with the man. It's not what's *there* that counts, it's what's projected—and . . . it's not what *he* projects but rather what the voter receives. It's not the man we have to change, but rather the received impression" (Kelly, *New York Times Magazine,* October 31, 1993, p. 67).

Familiar? Keeping the press at bay, limiting access to the candidate, arranging town hall meetings with friendly audiences and friendlier questions, fashioning the soundbite for the TV evening news, creating effective political ads, refusing to debate, taking few risks—this was the strategy, and Nixon won, beating Hubert Humphrey by a scant 0.7 percent of the vote. Nixon got 43.4 percent, Humphrey 42.7 percent, and third-party candidate George Wallace 13.5 percent.

Much of what the American public has come to distrust in modern-day campaigning, much of what ultimately came to rupture the electoral bond between the people and their government during the 1980s, started with Nixon in his 1968 run for the presidency.

Once he had achieved the power of incumbency, Nixon decided that he could finally move against the press. On March 2, 1970, he fired off a series of press directives to Haldeman. One of them called for "an all-out, slam-bang attack on the fact that the news people are overwhelmingly for Muskie, Kennedy, any liberal position . . . I want a game plan on my desk" (Kutler 1990, p. 163). Nixon wanted action. He was already convinced that the White House press corps was no different from any other press corps— liberal, pushy, determined to crush him and his agenda. News, by Nixon's definition, was what he said, not what reporters interpreted him as saying. He ordered his staff to treat the press with "the courteous, cool contempt which has been my policy over the last few years." He seemed to derive a perverse sense of satisfaction from his belief that the press hated him.

In March 1971 he told one reporter, "It is true that of all the Presidents in this century, it is probably true, that I have less, as somebody has said, supporters, in the press than any President." He added, "I'm one of the most hated" (Kutler 1990, p. 166).

He was convinced that a "solid majority" of 60–65 percent of the Washington press corps, the group that former Nixon chief of staff Alexander Haig once called "a strange and mysterious guild of moody misanthropes," approached any story "with a strong negative attitude toward RN." (1992, p. 198). Nixon felt that the press would "throw us a bone," but "their whole life objective is to bring us down." He told his staff in late 1972, when Watergate began to loom over the White House as a potentially debilitating problem, "The discrediting of the press must be our major objective over the next few months." (Kutler 1990, p. 175).

On one level Watergate was a battle between a president and a newspaper. Were it not for the reporting of the *Washington Post,* Watergate might have remained on the police blotter as a minor infraction, what spokesman Ziegler described as a "third-rate bur- glary attempt." But Bob Woodward and Carl Bernstein, two young metropolitan reporters, linked the burglary to the White House through exhaustive legwork—and through the under- standing support of editor Benjamin Bradlee and publisher Kath- arine Graham. For months, the Woodward and Bernstein exclu- sives were lonely outposts of journalistic courage. The *New York Times* tried but failed to match the *Post*'s coverage, and it took a while before CBS News began to contribute substantively to Watergate. In time, many other news organizations joined the hunt, as Congress and the courts accumulated evidence tying Nixon to the cover-up.

But on another level Watergate was a plunge into Nixon's psy- che—into what his aide Charles Colson described as "the dark side of our natures." It included, as one definition of Nixon's ap- proach to government, slush funds, hush money for thieves, forged cables, illegal wiretapping and break-ins by a secret "plumbers'" unit, and enemies lists, all this adding up to a flagrant abuse of presidential authority. From the Oval Office, Nixon lied to the press and to the American people, and he did so over and over again. He also demonstrated that he totally miscalculated the impact of Watergate on the country, Washington, and his career.

On June 21, 1972, Nixon told Haldeman, privately: "The reac- tion is going to be primarily in Washington and not the country, because I think the country doesn't give much of a shit about bug- ging when somebody bugs somebody else, you see. Everybody around here is all mortified about it. 'It's a terrible thing to bug.' Of course it isn't and most people around the country think it's probably routine, everybody's trying to bug everybody else. It's politics. That's my view. Now the purists probably won't agree with that, but I don't think you're going to see a great, great up-roar in the country about the Republican committee trying to bug the Democratic headquarters" (*Chicago Tribune,* "25 New Nixon Tapes are Made Public," May 17, 1993, p. 1).

Nixon lied in public, conceded the truth in private.

On August 22, 1972, Nixon said, publicly: "No one in the White House staff, no one in the administration, presently em-ployed, was involved in this very bizarre incident."

On March 22, 1973, Nixon said, privately: "I don't give a [exple-tive deleted] what happens. I want you all to stonewall it, let them plead the Fifth Amendment, cover up or anything else if it'll save the plan. That's the whole point." (The "plan" was to insulate the White House from any connection to Watergate.)

On August 15, 1973, Nixon said, publicly, "Not only was I un-aware of any cover-up, I was unaware there was anything to cover up" (*Washington Post,* June 14, 1992, pp. A21, A22, A23).

Public/private: the two sides of Nixon. Based on White House tapes still closeted away at the National Archives but seen and studied by the archivists, a portrait of Nixon has emerged from this period of his life. According to Seymour Hersh, writing in the December 14, 1992, issue of the *New Yorker:*

> The archivists found themselves appalled by Nixon's lack of character, by his emptiness. The tapes reveal not just that he was lonely or diffident; there seemed to be nothing inside. He had no real hobbies and no real friends. He was a man who would spend evening after evening in his office in the Executive Office Building, eating dinner alone, and telephoning aides to find out what "P.N."—his usual way of referring to his wife, Pat Nixon—was doing. His well-publicized friendship with Bebe Rebozo was empty: the two men would sit together for hours, sharing a few drinks, while Rebozo would tell the President,

"Keep it up" and "You're doing a great job" and "Your enemies are out to get you."

The tapes show him to be a racist. Pejorative words and phrases dominated much of his private talk: Jews were "kikes," blacks were "niggers," and reporters were "press pricks." Nixon's drinking was also unnerving; his problem was not that he drank too much but that he had very little capacity for handling liquor (pp. 93–94).

On August 9, 1974, Nixon ended his Watergate agony. He resigned. As he left the White House, he told hundreds of assembled guests: "We don't have a good word for it in English. But au revoir. We'll see you again." Then, with that characteristic gesture, both arms raised in an awkward V, Nixon boarded a White House helicopter and began his journey west.

Many people simply assumed, as did columnist David Broder, that after Nixon accepted a pardon from President Gerald Ford, he "might have the decency to live out his life in privacy" (*Washington Post,* April 23, 1994).

But within weeks after his resignation he began asking a few friends about whether—and how—he could restore his honor. They answered politely that books, articles, speeches, private memos, all stressing his command of foreign affairs, would help, but there was little conviction in their comments. They knew that there was no timetable, no road map, to renewed respectability, that it would be hard for anyone to come back from Watergate. They also knew that if Nixon were ever to reach this goal, it could only be with the help of the press— those who admired him and even those who "hated" him.

No one knew these ultimate truths about American politics better than Nixon. Though he was resolute, he was also in bad shape. A few months after his return to San Clemente, a politician so broken in spirit that Ziegler would later remark that he thought Nixon would simply end it all and "walk into the Pacific," the former president suffered a return visit of phlebitis, which required emergency surgery; his wife's childhood house was firebombed; and his psychological condition remained shaky. He needed months to recover his physical strength, years to overcome (if indeed he ever did) periodic bouts of depression.

Throughout this lengthy process, Nixon sought to restrict the flow of information about Watergate, and he largely succeeded. The White House tapes have been in the custody of the National Archives and Records Administration for many years. Nixon's lawyers used every legal detour to keep the bulk of the tapes from being made available to the American people. On August 4, 1993, they went to court yet again to stop the release of parts of thirty-nine conversations taped in July–August 1972 (Associated Press, August 4, 1993). Only sixty-three hours out of an estimated four thousand hours on 950 reels, or less than 2 percent of the reels, had been released to the public as of December 1992. By raising hundreds of objections and questions, his lawyers kept buying time, in the process inducing fratricidal warfare among archivists over such questions as Nixon's "right to privacy." Historian Stephen Ambrose has observed that there are "many methods" for controlling the release of government-held information, and "between 1977 and 1990 Nixon used every one of them" (Ambrose 1987, vol. 3, p. 503).

In this period of "ruin and recovery," Nixon often felt strapped for cash. He needed money for his lawyers and his family. It was a constant obsession. In August 1975, Nixon agreed to meet with British talk show host David Frost to discuss a series of television interviews. (He rejected all requests from U.S. anchors.) They settled on twelve two-hour sessions, leading to four ninety-minute broadcasts. Frost retained full editorial control, and Nixon received $600,000 and 20 percent of the profits, plus permission to draft his memoirs based in part on preparation for the TV interviews.

As he plunged into the task of writing *RN: The Memoirs of Richard Nixon,* which was ultimately published in early 1978 to mixed reviews, he would occasionally make a public appearance, testing the waters for reaction from the worlds of press and politics. In early 1975, he attended a GOP fundraiser in New York. It was his first political appearance and he was worried about timing. "I hope this isn't too soon," he told consultant Roger Stone (*Newsweek,* May 2, 1994, p. 30). In September 1975, as a guest of the Teamsters, who had supported him in the 1968 and 1972 campaigns, he attended a charity golf tournament, a bizarre decision that led to sharp criticism from the *New York Times* and other newspapers. Why would Nixon have chosen such a sponsor? The Teamsters at the time were being accused of links with Mafia mobsters. Stung by the criticism, Nixon retreated to San Clemente.

Four months later, Nixon emerged once again. On February 21, 1976, against the advice of both President Gerald Ford and Secretary of State Henry Kissinger, he went to Beijing on the fourth anniversary of his ground-breaking trip to China. Though held in disrepute at home, Nixon was honored as a statesman and former president in Communist China. He was received by China's leaders, and he spoke about U.S.–China relations. He made news. Ford, in the midst of the New Hampshire presidential primary, was obliged to answer questions about his controversial decision to pardon Nixon shortly after succeeding him in the White House. Ford was embarrassed. A June 1976 poll asked, "Do you think Ford did the right thing [in pardoning Nixon] or the wrong thing?" Fifty-five percent answered that Ford had done "the wrong thing" (*Newsweek,* June 14, 1982, p. 38).

In May 1977, "Nixon on Nixon" began to run on American television. The Frost interviews were roundly criticized. The questions were soft, the answers rambling and murky, but that was all irrelevant. Nixon was back on the tube.

Within a matter of six months, Nixon would also be back in Washington for his first visit since Watergate, but it was by an ironic route. On Christmas Eve, 1977, the Nixons were at home in San Clemente, both ill, depressed, and alone for the holidays, when a very sick Hubert Humphrey telephoned from Minnesota. The old warrior of the Democratic Party, reduced to a frail shell by cancer, was calling many of his political friends and foes to say goodbye. He knew that he did not have much time. His conversation with Nixon troubled him, and a few days later he again called the man who had defeated him by a whisker in the presidential race of 1968. Humphrey invited Nixon to attend his funeral service in Washington. Humphrey said that he had made all of the arrangements: he wanted Nixon to stand in a place of honor reserved for a former president.

Humphrey died on January 13, 1978. Two days later, his funeral service was held in Washington. One of Humphrey's closest friends, Paul Rexford Thatcher Sr., later recalled that "to the surprise of most and the gasps of many," he had welcomed Nixon to the Capitol Rotunda and escorted him "to the place of honor with the others, near the flag-draped casket" (*Washington Post,* January 20, 1993, op-ed p. A21). If the positions had been reversed, would a dying Nixon have called a political adversary on Christmas Eve? Would he, from the grave, have made sure that Humphrey stood in a place of honor?

In the summer of 1978, a few months after the publication of *RN,* Nixon made two domestic trips—the first to Hyden, Kentucky, the second to Biloxi, Mississippi. In both places, he was received warmly, press coverage was generally friendly, and he began to think about widening his travel horizons.

Nixon, in November, went to France and England. He learned, much to his delight, that Watergate was only a receding curiosity in Western Europe. There corruption at the highest levels of government was so commonly associated with "politics" that it was hardly worth a fuss.

At the Oxford Union, Nixon was received with jeers outside (principally, he thought, from American students) but with a standing ovation inside. "It was no cakewalk," Nixon would later write. Questions were blunt, even irreverent, "but unlike many university audiences in the United States today, they did not try to shout the speaker down. They wanted to hear what he had to say." Nixon got what he considered an "extremely favorable reception." He offered three reasons. "The students liked the fact that I spoke without notes; they thought that I was giving my own views rather than reading a canned speech that others had written for me. They particularly liked the question-and-answer period, which was filled with tough questions and equally tough rejoinders. Above all, they were serious students of world affairs" (Nixon, *In the Arena,* pp. 46–47).

Nixon was particularly pleased by one question, which, he claimed, was "unexpected." Did his plans include a return to American politics? "I responded that my political career was over but that while I had retired from politics, I had not retired from life. I concluded my answer by saying, 'So long as I have a breath in my body, I am going to talk about the great issues that affect the world. I am not going to keep my mouth shut. I am going to speak out for peace and freedom'" (*In the Arena,* p. 47).

In Paris, Nixon was invited to do a three-hour interview on French television. He accepted and performed brilliantly, according to a number of reviews. American reporters speculated that he was preparing a return to active politics. "They were right in one respect but wrong in another," he wrote. "I was indeed launching a campaign, but not for a personal comeback, which would have been both unrealistic and, even more important, contrary to my real goal. I had spent thirty years of my life studying and acting in the area of foreign policy. I had some unique experience and had developed some strong views about the mistakes that had been made in the past and the need for new policies in the future. I wanted to share those experiences and those views with others who had responsibilities for making or affecting the decisions that would make a difference in the world scene" (*In the Arena,* pp. 47–48).

Except for one part of his explanation, there was no reason to be skeptical about his story. Nixon did have extensive experience in foreign policy, but the main reason he wanted to share it—to write and lecture about it—was that he believed it was the best way of putting distance between himself and Watergate.

In January 1979, Nixon returned to the White House for the first time since Watergate. However brief the visit, it was, for him, exhilarating. President Jimmy Carter had invited him to a state dinner honoring Chinese leader Deng Xiaoping. It was Deng's idea, not Carter's, but no matter. Within a few weeks, Nixon announced that he would be making another trip to Beijing in September, and a Gallup poll listed the former president as one of the ten most admired Americans. Two years before, he had been listed as one of the ten most despised Americans.

In February 1980, believing that he was ready for another step up the ladder of rehabilitation, Nixon moved to New York, as he had done in the mid-1960s, claiming that he and Pat had been "dying" in California, presumably of boredom. Even if New York's opinion leaders were not yet ready for Nixon, he was ready for them. He moved into a brownstone on East 65th Street and attempted to hire GOP political pro Edward Rollins as his chief of staff. (Rollins stayed with the victorious Reagan campaign.)

In March, Nixon was off to France again and then on to Africa. In May, his next book, *Real War*, was published, and it became an immediate best-seller in the tense atmosphere of the Iran hostage crisis. It conveyed an alarmist, almost apocalyptic, vision of the United States and the Soviet Union locked in a fight to the finish, foreshadowing Ronald Reagan's "Evil Empire" speech and policy.

In September, Nixon gave an interview to Theodore H. White, which was published in *Parade* magazine, and then, for a whole week, appeared on NBC's "Today" program, commenting on the presidential campaign and portraying himself in passing as a "senior statesman." He explained that he was receiving twenty to thirty requests for press interviews every week. Watergate would occasionally be raised, of course, and Nixon would acknowledge a "mistake," but the thrust of these interviews was polite inquiry into his views about politics, diplomacy, and sports. The press seemed as eager as Nixon to softpedal Watergate.

Buoyed by the increasingly favorable press coverage and positively elated by conservative Ronald Reagan's victory in November 1980, Nixon felt comfortable enough to extend his political reach in the Republican Party. He wrote a confidential, eleven-page memo to the president-elect on November 17, 1990 (Smith 1991, p. 38). Whether in the transition crush the memo ever reached Reagan's desk is less meaningful than what the memo reflected about Nixon's style and attitude at the time. He wanted to establish his credentials as a reliable and available confidant.

He reassured Reagan: "As far as my own personal situation is concerned, I do not, as you know, seek any official position. However, I would welcome the opportunity to provide advice in areas where I have special experience to you and to members of your

Cabinet and the White House staff where you deem it appropriate."

Six years after Watergate, Nixon was ready to play the role of presidential adviser. With Reagan, he succeeded, at least to some extent. John Lehman, then Secretary of the Navy, recalled that Nixon was "the guiding intellectual hand of the Reagan foreign policy. . . . Reagan really listened to him, because he always had something original to say" (*U.S. News & World Report,* May 2, 1994, p. 35). Even if Reagan listened, it was not always clear that he grasped the import of Nixon's advice or that he took it. No matter. The impression grew that Nixon was beginning to make an impact.

The press continued to give him extensive exposure. In early 1981, *New York* magazine published a bold cover with the words "He's Back!" emblazoned across a picture of Nixon. And indeed the former president was back—hosting a series of dinners for publishers, politicians, and reporters, including Hugh Sidey of *Time* and Leonard Garment, a former law partner who had worked for him in the White House. Roger Stone, a tough-minded political operative from the Reagan campaign, suggested that Nixon "very selectively" invite young, "unbiased" reporters to a separate round of private dinners. "Unbiased" was defined as a journalist who had not covered Watergate or one who seemed sympathetic. On this list were Morton Kondracke of the *New Republic,* Strobe Talbott and Roger Rosenblatt of *Time,* Sara Fritz of the *Los Angeles Times,* Gerald Boyd of the *New York Times,* and others (Michael Beschloss, *Vanity Fair,* June 1992, p. 118).

According to Beschloss, many of these journalists were charmed by Nixon's wit and insights, a few were repelled by his style. One of them later recalled for Beschloss: "His eyes fluttered and his face tightened at the slightest interruption, the slightest back talk. There was something so obviously rehearsed, calculating, unspontaneous about the whole thing. We were being played like violins and we knew it."

Nixon also invited well-connected Republicans to New Jersey for one-on-one-briefings: Tom Korologos, a former aide in his White House, on congressional matters; Herb Stein, once chairman of his Council of Economic Advisers, on economic developments; and former ambassadors James Lilley and Vernon Walters, on international affairs (*U.S. News & World Report,* May 2, 1994, p. 35).

In July 1981, the White House beckoned once again. Anwar Sadat, who had signed a historic peace treaty with Israel only a few years before, was assassinated by Moslem fundamentalists in Cairo, and Reagan organized a very high level U.S. delegation to the funeral, including former presidents Ford, Carter—and Nixon, who quickly accepted. Though the occasion was somber, Nixon appreciated the invitation, for it suggested that he was now considered to be on an equal footing with other former presidents.

In 1982, another book, *Leaders,* was published. It was syndicated nationally and internationally by the *New York Times,* and it also climbed to the best-seller lists. Nixon wrote about political leaders who had impressed him over the years. He included only one American—Douglas MacArthur, the flamboyant general fired by President Harry Truman in 1951 for "open defiance" of his orders. Truman, backed by the Joint Chiefs of Staff, described MacArthur's action in his memoirs as "a challenge to the President under the Constitution." Then-Senator Nixon demanded MacArthur's immediate reinstatement amidst GOP calls for Truman's impeachment (McCullough 1992, p. 837).

With his now-substantial profits from books and syndication

rights, Nixon bought a spacious home in Saddle River, New Jersey. He delivered dozens of speeches, wrote op-ed pieces, addressed editorial boards "on background," courted journalists, and traveled from one end of the world to the other, meeting world leaders and discussing global issues. He visited every country in Eastern Europe, except Poland and East Germany. In China, he reviewed reforms with Deng Xiaoping. (Communist countries always rolled out the red carpet for Nixon.) In London, he toured the diplomatic horizon with Prime Minister Margaret Thatcher.

Toward the end of 1982, Nixon got a "Dear Mr. President" letter from Talbott of *Time,* then a diplomatic reporter, requesting an interview. Nixon had already been courting Talbott and decided to reestablish his old working relationship with the magazine that then had the largest circulation of all the newsweeklies. Nixon, whose early anti–"Red China" passion had made him a *Time* favorite back in the 1950s, agreed to do the interview. (By the time of his death, Nixon had been the subject of a *Time* cover story fifty-six times, a record no one else may ever eclipse [*Time,* May 2, 1994, p. 4].)

Nixon prepared "meticulously," Talbott told me. "I was tantalized by the idea that, though he was still a non-person, he'd make a great interview." Though Nixon set no ground rules, it quickly became apparent that he was "on the record," meaning everything he said could be quoted. Talbott lost no time and pulled a notebook out of his pocket, and, as rapidly as Nixon spoke, Talbott wrote. The interview, which appeared in the December 27, 1982, issue of *Time,* focused on Nixon's evolving views about U.S. policy toward the Soviet Union. With Yuri Andropov's ascent to power following Leonid Brezhnev's death, Nixon recommended that President Reagan moderate his rigid anti-Communism and seek better relations with the Soviet Union. "From everything I know," Nixon said, "Andropov is a smarter, more imaginative breed of Soviet leader." (In an April 22, 1985, issue of *Time,* a year after Andropov's death, Nixon took a far less positive view. "When Andropov came along, I practically lost my breakfast when I read some of that sappy stuff about him in the morning papers—how he liked Western pop music and so on.")

Nixon worried that relations between the superpowers were getting too dangerous. Talbott quoted him as saying: "Right now, we're frozen into the ice so tightly that we may get to the point where only a bomb can blast us out. A conflict in China or the Middle East or any place could lead to the ultimate disaster. We've got to avoid that." While not attacking Reagan directly, Nixon criticized the administration's underlying conviction that military pressure could bring the Soviet Union to its knees. Nixon said: "There's a school of thought that hard-line policies on our part will induce change for the better on their part. I wish that were the case, but it's just not going to happen." Ironically, by the late 1980s, many observers not ordinarily identified with the Reagan right credited his "hard-line policies" with undermining Moscow's vulnerable economy and thus helping to bring about the end of the Cold War.

Those seeking absolute consistency in Nixon's approach to Communist countries are bound to be disappointed. He was often pragmatic, always opportunistic, and rarely ideological. Principle was not crucial. He was capable of using the right wing rallying cry "Who lost China?" to pillory the Democrats and advance his own political fortunes during his rise to the presidency and then once in office of launching a period of détente, signing arms control agreements with Moscow and reopening relations with Beijing. As president, Nixon worried about survival

in the nuclear age. He was prepared to confront the devil or cooperate with the devil, depending on the challenge.

At this moment in U.S.–Soviet relations, he thought that
Reagan's vision of the Soviet Union was outdated and that the
United States ought to adopt a far more nuanced and sophisticated policy toward a country that had tens of thousands of nuclear weapons targeted on American cities.

In the summer of 1983, Nixon experimented with a new tech-
nique in political public relations and persuasion that he was to
use again in 1992, when he circulated the memo critical of Bush's
policy on aid to Russia. At his own expense, he published *Real
Peace,* a short, urgent book on U.S.–Soviet relations. In late August, he mailed 115 bound copies with a brief covering letter to a
list of national and world leaders and prominent journalists,
among them Reagan, Kissinger, Thatcher, François Mitterand,
George Shultz, Sidey, William F. Buckley, Jr., and William Safire.
Seven hundred copies were later sent to a broader group of leaders, including members of Congress and the press. He could have
written an op-ed piece or accepted an invitation to appear on television, but instead he chose this unusual route to express his view
that the old hard-line approach to Russia had to be moderated in
light of the changes in Moscow's leadership. Nixon seemed to believe that the message of *Real Peace* would be taken more seriously
and attract more attention if it was placed between hard covers.
By seeding the political environment in Washington and New
York with many copies of this "forbidden fruit," a book that could
not be bought in a store but had to be received in the mail, giving
it a very special cachet, Nixon was hoping to generate private and
public discussion that would end up pressuring the White House
into changing its policy toward the Soviet Union.

Whether it was Nixon's calculated pressure that moved President Reagan to soften the tone of his anti-Soviet policy in January,

1984, at the start of his reelection campaign, or whether Reagan, under parallel pressure from his wife, Nancy, had intended to change his image in any case, the administration's policy toward the Soviet Union suddenly shifted.

I remember the time well. I had not received a copy of *Real Peace*. I had only heard about it at a Washington dinner party. It took several days before I could persuade a friend to lend me the copy he had gotten "confidentially" from the former president. My friend wondered whether he was doing the right thing. He did not understand that Nixon would have approved of this "leak," though perhaps not of the journalist to whom it was leaked. The whole point was to disseminate his views.

In 1984, as another presidential campaign began, Nixon arranged a television memoir, for which he received $1 million. CBS purchased U.S. rights for $500,000 and aired the memoir on April 8, 10, and 15. It broke no new ground. On other TV programs, Nixon engaged in one of his favorite pastimes—that of predicting political outcomes. He was not always right. He predicted, for example, that the Democratic ticket would consist of Walter Mondale and Gary Hart and that the race would be a close one. As it turned out, Mondale and his running mate Geraldine Ferraro were overwhelmed by a Republican landslide.

Nixon was particularly pleased by the reaction to his appearance on May 9 before the American Society of Newspaper Editors. He had been invited to the vipers' nest, and he had been given a standing ovation. "I have no enemies in the press whatsoever," he proclaimed. For every reporter who remembered Watergate, it seemed that there were dozens of editors who wanted either to forget the scandal or to put it in "historical perspective." They seemed eager to convey the impression to the former president that though they might have participated in covering his downfall, they held no personal grudges. By their smiles and handshakes, they were trying to say that they were professionals—editors and reporters who were simply covering the news. When Watergate, as a national crisis, ended, they moved on to other stories.

The next morning, the headline in the *New York Times* read, "Nixon Wins Applause from Newspaper Editors." The *Washington Post* was more laudatory. The headline on its story read, "Nixon's Candor and Humor Stop the Press." A few days later, the *Post* ran long excerpts from Nixon's speech over two pages of its Sunday edition.

Nineteen eighty-five saw the publication of *No More Vietnams,* his sixth book and fifth since Watergate. It was an apologia, filled with historical inaccuracies, but it still moved rapidly up the bestseller lists. Nixon had become to books about politics what Robert Ludlum had become to books about espionage. The *Times* and the *Post* published devastating reviews; conservative journals praised the book. Nixon confidently stuck to the theme that next time the United States faced a Vietnam-type crisis, it should unleash its military power—and win!

By this time, Nixon had become hot copy. He was being approached by journalists not just for new or old insights into his presidency but for more general insights into history. He had moved from politician to oracle in editorial offices around the country. His friends at *Time* asked him for an eight-thousand-word essay on the fortieth anniversary of Hiroshima. *Foreign Affairs* asked for an article on summitry. He began researching his next book, and he traveled endlessly—to Japan, China again, South Korea, Hong Kong, Singapore, Malaysia, and Thailand. (He never set foot in Taiwan, because he did not want to offend Communist China.) Everywhere he was received with the respect reserved for former presidents.

Rolling Stone, not exactly the kind of publication that would choose to extol the virtues of Richard M. Nixon, started 1986 with an eye-catching list called "Who's Hot: New Stars in Your Future." You guessed it: Richard Nixon was a "new star" on the list. In April 1986, Nixon wowed the annual get-together of newspaper publishers and won another standing ovation for his review of global politics. Katharine Graham of the *Washington Post* shook his hand and recommended to the editors of *Newsweek,* another of her journalistic properties, that they do a major spread on him. A recommendation from Graham was the equivalent of a direct order. When the issue appeared, Nixon was on the cover and the headline shouted, "He's Back: The Rehabilitation of Nixon." Inside were six pages of articles, twelve photos, and a three-page interview with "The Sage of Saddle River."

Over the next several years, Nixon moved resolutely toward higher and higher levels of political acceptability. If Watergate was not exactly forgotten, it was no longer front and center in the nation's political memory. Nixon operated on the theory that the American people had a short attention span and a forgiving nature, especially with respect to the moral lapses of former presidents. His comeback trail was studded with journalistic opportunities, books, travel, and the cultivation of old and new political contacts, including the following:

—a visit in July 1986 with Soviet leader Mikhail Gorbachev in Moscow, his first trip to the Soviet capital since 1974, the year he resigned from the presidency;

—the writing of dozens of op-ed pieces, principally in the *New York Times,* the *Los Angeles Times,* and *Time* magazine;

—three more books—his seventh, eighth, and ninth: *1999: Victory without War,* published in 1988; *In the Arena: A Memoir of Victory, Defeat and Renewal,* published in 1990; and *Seize the*

Moment, America's Challenge in a One-Superpower World, published in 1992;

—a special one-hour appearance on "Meet the Press" on April 10, 1988, during which he acknowledged that he had been wrong to cover up the Watergate scandal and lamented that he had not really been tough enough on the North Vietnamese;

—a controversial visit to Beijing after the Tiananmen crackdown in early June 1989, after which he met with President Bush;

—an unusual Washington visit on March 8, 1990, described by Senator Robert Dole as his "rehabilitation," during which Nixon spoke to a House GOP conference and held a news conference;

—in May 1990, a series of television interviews with Bryant Gumble on NBC and Morton Kondracke on PBS;

—the dedication of the Nixon Library on July 19, 1990, a media event attended by Presidents Ford, Reagan, and Bush; each gushed with praise for Nixon, and Nixon responded with a call for risk taking: "If you take no risks, you will suffer no defeats. But without risks, you will win no victories. You must never be satisfied with success, and you should never be discouraged by failure. Failure can be sad. But the greatest sadness is not to try and fail, but to fail to try at all. Only when you become engaged in a cause greater than yourself, can you be true to yourself."

The great cause that came to engage Nixon's attention in 1992, and that was to be his last challenge, was the development of a major aid program for Russia. No other cause, in his view, was more urgent. How to stimulate democracy? How to encourage a free market system? How to control thousands of nuclear warheads? He bent all of his efforts toward helping Russia. He used the press, he used old and new political contacts, he used the American presidency, whether represented by Republican George Bush or Democrat Bill Clinton, and he used all of his cunning, guile, and skill.

This ambitious goal went hand in glove with Nixon's larger goal of personal recovery from Watergate. What is clear is that this aging politician, no matter how he was packaged, old, new, newer, newest, disgraced, or rehabilitated, eager even at his age for another round of adulation, for another contribution to his country, absolutely convinced that he ranked with Churchill, de Gaulle, and Roosevelt as one of the giants of the twentieth century— Richard Nixon was determined not to be forgotten. By focusing U.S. and Western attention on an aid package for Russia, he found the way.

3

"TO GIVE HISTORY A NUDGE"

After decades of denouncing Communism at home and abroad, Richard Nixon did not rise one wintry day in February 1992, and shout, "Eureka! The U.S. must urgently send billions of dollars of aid to Russia!" Indeed, until August 1991, he had staunchly resisted the idea, promoted by Americans impressed by Gorbachev's reforms. He argued as late as the spring of that year that until a Soviet leader renounced Communism and embraced the concepts of democracy and a market economy, massive aid would amount to little more than what he called "counterproductive Western painkillers" (*Washington Post,* June 2, 1991, p. D1).

Then, on August 19, a botched right wing coup, surely one of the strangest in modern history, touched off a dramatic chain of events and Nixon began to change his mind. The first day, the old-line Communist coup leaders, nervous, drunk, without a coherent plan of action, sent tanks rolling into central Moscow. They took up attack positions around Boris Yeltsin's headquarters, the parliament building, known as the "White House." A small crowd of his supporters gathered outside. CNN broadcast the scene around the world. Foreign chanceries held their collective breath. Would Russia's retreat from Communism be allowed to continue? Suddenly a defiant Yeltsin climbed on top of one of the tanks. He denounced the "anti-constitutional coup d'état" and called on Russia's citizens to resist the plotters. At that moment Yeltsin emerged unmistakably as the leader of another Russian revolution. By evening some twenty-five thousand citizens had gathered at the White House to defend their elected government with homemade barricades. The troops—and the generals—wavered. For three days the tense standoff continued, and then, miraculously, the tanks pulled out of Moscow.

Gorbachev, after four days of house arrest in the Crimea, returned to Moscow a broken man. His wife, the once proud, self-assured Raisa, seemed a frightened shadow of her former self. Though Gorbachev did not immediately abdicate power, he must have understood that power, like sand, was running through his fingers and accumulating in Yeltsin's hands. It took another four months before Gorbachev formally quit and Yeltsin assumed control of the Kremlin. Communism, as an official, governing philosophy, died in the Soviet Union. The great "social experiment" of the twentieth century, pushed by such revolutionaries as Lenin, Stalin, Mao, and Castro, survived only in Cuba and China—and in forms that the founders would not have recognized. The Soviet Union disintegrated into fifteen separate countries. The Cold War ended.

Only at that point did Nixon drop his former reservations and decide to launch a major campaign to help post-Communist Russia. At the center of his strategy was the drafting of his very controversial memo critical of President Bush.

Like many other observers of the international scene, Nixon had been fascinated by the changes brought to the Soviet Union by Gorbachev, who came to power in March 1985 after the deaths of three elderly leaders in the space of three years. Nixon sensed a reordering of Soviet society but was still so rooted in his old doubts and suspicions about the Communists that he was initially unable to appreciate the profound nature of the changes.

When Gorbachev met with Reagan at a get-acquainted summit

in Geneva in November 1985, the smiles and handshakes before a roaring fire ignited a period of high expectations. Nixon, who had earlier urged Reagan to moderate his anti-Soviet stance, now expressed the fear that Reagan might be going too far. On March 6, 1986, in an address to the Los Angeles World Affairs Council, Nixon warned about "the soft illusion of mutual affection"and pressed instead for "the hard reality of mutual respect" (*Los Angeles Times,* March 7, 1986, p. 4).

Speaking before a sellout crowd of more than a thousand people, Nixon called for "a new realism" in U.S.–Soviet relations built on eight "pillars of peace."

1. The Soviet Union, as a military superpower, "deserves our respect." He continued: "Affection between allies is useful. Respect between adversaries is indispensable."
2. Profound differences between the two superpowers remain. Resolve differences when possible; when it is not possible, avoid "dying over them."
3. The United States should not impose capitalism on the Soviet Union, and if the Soviet Union attempts to impose Communism on us or on our allies, we must resist.
4. The United States should not seek to achieve "military superiority" over the Soviet Union, nor should the Soviet Union be allowed to achieve such superiority over the United States.
5. The United States should meet the Soviet Union "halfway" to "defuse Third World conflicts in areas where our interests collide in such a way that they could draw us into war."
6. Both superpowers should confront the common enemy of international terrorism.
7. The United States should attempt to increase trade with the Soviet Union.

8. Finally, in an effort to modernize his old policy of "détente," he proposed that "we should break new ground by combining competition and coexistence. We should compete with each other economically and ideologically on both sides of the Iron Curtain."

In effect, Nixon was outlining new guidelines for what his old nemesis, Nikita Khrushchev, used to call "peaceful coexistence." Nothing in his speech suggested an awareness that the Soviet Union was on the edge of economic and political collapse. Quite the contrary. During the Gorbachev years, Nixon felt that the Soviet Union was still a virile, if somewhat troubled, superpower that had to be confronted in a more sophisticated way.

Toward the end of June 1986, Nixon returned to Moscow for the first time in twelve years. He was accompanied by one aide, John Taylor, and the visit was described as "private," though he had conferred with Reagan before leaving. Nixon addressed the Institute on the U.S.A. and Canada, a Moscow think tank run by academician Georgy Arbatov, a well-traveled expert on the United States. On July 14, Nixon met for two and a half hours with Andrei Gromyko, the figurehead president of the Soviet Union who had served for decades as a tough, unyielding foreign minister. Nixon was angling for a meeting with Gorbachev. On July 16, Nixon had a working lunch with Anatoly Dobrynin, who had been Soviet ambassador to Washington for many years and who now served as Gorbachev's senior adviser on foreign affairs. Later Taylor was asked by reporters if a Gorbachev-Nixon meeting had been arranged. "President Nixon has no such plans at this time," responded the Nixon aide. "We have made no such request."

The phrase "at this time" should have alerted reporters to the imminence of the meeting. The following day, literally hours before Nixon's planned departure, he and Gorbachev met at the Kremlin for "a frank and detailed conversation." The Soviet news agency TASS reported, contrary to what Taylor had said, that it was Nixon who had requested the meeting. Dobrynin was the only other person present. Nixon refused to discuss details with the press, claiming that he had promised Reagan, then in the early stages of arranging another summit with Gorbachev, that he would report on the content of his meetings only to the president. This mum's-the-word approach served to keep the spotlight on Nixon, which was exactly where he wanted it.

Over the next few years, Gorbachev rocketed to international acclaim. He dismantled the worst features of the Soviet state, unleashing a peaceful revolution in a country so vast that it occupied one-sixth of the land surface of the world. The established order of things began to crumble. The Communist Party and bureaucracy could not keep up with the rapid change. The economy collapsed. The nationalities problem deepened, as fighting erupted among different ethnic groups. The East European empire disintegrated. The Red Army lost its edge, as troop withdrawals encouraged a rush of desertions. Still, Gorbachev had the knack, at least in those days, of keeping many balls in the air at the same time. When he sensed that his domestic flank was weakening, he returned to the world stage for another dazzling performance.

In December 1988, Gorbachev went to the United Nations and delivered an exceptional address to the General Assembly. He announced a dramatic, unilateral reduction in the Soviet military, specifically a cut of 500,000 troops and 10,000 tanks over a short period of time. At a U.N. reception, the ebullient Soviet leader radiated confidence and charisma, charming one and all, including Nixon. The former president, in those years, seemed occasionally to be at war with his past instincts about the Soviet Union, allowing himself to be beguiled by Gorbachev one minute and wary of him the next.

"We [must] keep our minds open to the possibility of far-reaching reform in the Soviet system," Nixon said, reflecting a cautious line he was to take in a number of op-ed pieces. At the same time he stressed that it would be a "mistake" to "buy" the "common Soviet ploy" that Gorbachev is a "moderate beset by conservative rivals." Nixon seemed more comfortable as the skeptic than as the optimist. Gorbachev, he wrote, "more than his predecessors, is a powerful reminder that we underestimate the Soviets at our peril" and that, far from representing the "end of the U.S.–Soviet rivalry," the Gorbachev era actually represented the "beginning of a dangerous, challenging new stage of the struggle between the superpowers" (*Chicago Tribune*, March 20, 1988, section 4, p. 4).

It was indeed to be a "new stage" in the East-West struggle, but not in the way that Nixon had envisaged. By March 1991, Gorbachev was "beset by conservative rivals" in the Communist Party, the KGB, and the Red Army, and he seemed to be losing his grip. Nixon felt that another trip to Moscow would be instructive. It would be organized by the well-connected Dimitri Simes, a Russian émigré working at the Carnegie Endowment for International Peace who, according to Morton Abramowitz, president of the Endowment, played a major role in the evolution of Nixon's thinking about the Soviet Union during this period.

Simes had arrived in the United States during the Nixon presidency. His parents were prominent Moscow attorneys who defended Jewish dissidents before joining their son in the United States in 1978. For a time there was a dark suspicion in some Western intelligence circles that Simes had to be some sort of Soviet agent, but there was never any evidence and before long he came to be recognized in Washington as an impressive foreign policy analyst with extraordinary contacts in both worlds. He had the additional virtue, useful to journalists, of being able to explain complicated matters of policy in simple sentences or soundbites and to write op-ed pieces under tight deadline. Simes, like so many others in Washington, was driven by a sharp sense of ambition and a determination to affect public policy.

The Nixon-Simes association had begun in 1984, when, on the tenth anniversary of Nixon's resignation, Simes wrote an op-ed piece in the *Christian Science Monitor* praising Nixon's wisdom and courage in the conduct of foreign affairs while at the same time observing that it was his unprincipled aides whose actions had undermined and ultimately corrupted his presidency. Nixon, flattered by Simes's sympathetic interpretation of the Watergate scandal, warned jocularly in a brief note of thanks that Simes's colleagues at Carnegie would surely not approve of his views. Nixon and Simes then began exchanging letters on various aspects of U.S.–Soviet relations. Shortly after Gorbachev's rise to power in 1985, Taylor called Simes and arranged a meeting with Nixon at a Washington hotel. A professional friendship quickly developed. "I like him very much," Simes told me. "I feel genuinely loyal to him. I've always been impressed by his grace, his friendship, how nice he is to associates."

Nixon's trip in March–April 1991 was his seventh to the Soviet Union since his famous "kitchen debate" with Khrushchev in August 1959. He remarked, during a stroll through Moscow's Central Market, "I never expected to make another trip. I probably will not be back. Age and everything." Nixon toured Lithuania, Georgia, and Ukraine. Wherever he went, he saw everyone who was anyone—leaders of the Communist Party, members of the rising political opposition. Few foreign visitors from government, academia, or the press had had such access in recent years. Overall he met, according to Simes, with thirty-two senior officials, including Gorbachev and Yeltsin. Yeltsin had broken away from the Communist Party to emerge as the second most powerful politician in the country. As chairman of the Russian parliament, elected by the members, he had become the leader of a group of liberal reformers impatient with Gorbachev's indecisiveness. With exquisite symmetry, Simes organized ninety-minute meetings with each contender to the Russian throne. Then, instead of holding a news conference before his departure, Nixon met with three American reporters to discuss his reaction to the burning question of the hour: could Gorbachev survive? (The reporters were Serge Schmemann of the *New York Times,* David Remnick of the *Washington Post,* and Jeff Trimble of *U.S. News & World Report.*)

"I am not among those," Nixon told them, "who believe we're going to see Gorbachev leave the scene anytime soon. The reason is that he is a brilliant politician. He is a competitor, no question about that. He acquired power. He likes power. He intends to keep it. He's a fighter" (Serge Schmemann, *New York Times,* April 4, 1991, p. 4). David Remnick chose another Nixon quote. "I just don't think he's finished. I don't see that. It's that point they make of whether there was the 'old Nixon' or the 'new Nixon.' Well, is it the 'old Gorbachev' or the 'new Gorbachev'? We liked the old one. Is there a new one? He says he's the same one." Nixon then added, for emphasis: "The question is, what is the alternative? . . . I don't see one" (David Remnick, *Washington Post,* April 4, 1991, p. 1).

Nixon did see a difference in Gorbachev. "The bouncy spirit that I saw particularly in 1988 [at the U.N. reception in New York] and the confidence I saw in 1986 was not as evident this time," he told the reporters. "This is a man with the weight of the world and his country on his shoulders. I don't mean to say he sounds depressed, there's nothing of that. There's no emotional problem there ... but I would say that he was tired—not physically, but just tired from the tremendous burden."

Then Nixon compared Gorbachev to Yeltsin. "This man is not a lightweight. I'd say this: Gorbachev is Wall Street and Yeltsin is Main Street. Gorbachev is Georgetown drawing rooms and Yeltsin is Newark factory gate. I can see where Yeltsin has enormous appeal as a political leader. He could become, if he had the desire to do so, the leader of a violent revolution." He continued: "But the fact is, this has been a peaceful opposition in Russia, and that is a credit to Gorbachev, but also a credit to Yeltsin. Yeltsin is one who could be a revolutionary leader; he could charge people up. He has the animal magnetism. I also think he has the ruthlessness. But curiously enough, I doubt that Yeltsin wants Gorbachev's job." Nixon was right about Yeltsin's potential as a Kremlin leader, which he was to become in a few months, but wrong about his lack of interest in replacing Gorbachev.

"There is at present no alternative to Gorbachev," Nixon concluded. "In terms of a leader, neither the reformers on the left nor the reactionaries, none of them really have a candidate that is an alternative to Gorbachev at this time, and I see no one who is in his league."

When Nixon returned to the United States in April 1991, he reported his impressions to President Bush, lectured at the Carnegie Endowment, and then retreated to his home in New Jersey to finish a book about a proper American response to the changes in Russia.

It was at this time that a Harvard professor named Graham Allison and a Russian economist named Gregori Yavlinsky began to go public with a bold, three-part plan of action for aid to Russia. Helping in the conceptualization of the plan was Robert Blackwill, a lecturer in public policy at the Kennedy School of Government and former White House foreign policy adviser during the Bush administration. It focused, first, on a radical devolution of authority from Moscow and the Communist Party to local political organizations; second, on democratization (including a specific timetable for local and national elections); and third, on the emergence of a market economy (bits and pieces of which were already beginning to come into play). Allison and Yavlinsky knew that their plan would cost billions, and they set about trying to sell it to the press, the White House, Congress, and the G-7, the group of seven Western economic leaders who were then preparing for a July summit in London. Allison and Yavlinsky believed that, in order to implement their plan, substantial quantities of economic and humanitarian aid, perhaps as much as $30 billion a year over a period of five years, would have to be sent to Russia. They stressed that this Western aid would be linked directly to Soviet performance: meaning, if the Russians did not advance toward democratization and a free market, they would not get the money; if they did advance toward these goals, they would get the money—and a lot more, in the form of Peace Corps volunteers, agricultural experts, political scientists, and technological expertise.

This rather sophisticated concept, once it was explained to the press by Allison and Yavlinsky, was quickly labeled the "grand bargain." According to Allison, the press "exaggerated" and "misrepresented" the plan. Allison said that, by referring to it as the "grand bargain," the press encouraged a number of conservatives in or near the Bush administration to criticize and distort it as a "grand giveaway." While it was true that the press fastened on to the "grand bargain" as an eye-catching headline, a journalistic shortcut for explaining a complicated plan, it was also true that Allison, Blackwill, and Yavlinsky all used the phrase in their press interviews to attract more attention and interest. And they succeeded. In trips to Washington, Tokyo, and West European capitals, they were frequently interviewed on television and their explanations appeared on many op-ed pages.

Among those who saw and read Allison and Yavlinsky was Nixon, and his initial reaction was strongly negative. In an op-ed piece in the *Washington Post* on June 2, 1991, Nixon criticized and belittled the Allison/Yavlinsky plan as a "Western bailout." "Some have touted the proposed $100 billion aid package as a 'grand bargain,'" he wrote. "But a 'grand con job' sounds like a more appropriate term."

He continued: "Since the Soviet Union only reforms when under pressure, a helping hand would hinder the cause of democracy. Although they are on the ropes, the forces of reaction are not down and out. They will exploit Western aid to preserve the Communist system, even if only in a modified form."

Nixon set three preconditions for aid. Otherwise, aid, in his judgment, made no strategic sense. First, there had to be a "geopolitical accommodation." Although East-West relations had improved under Gorbachev, a further easing of international tension was required, including a new strategic arms reduction treaty and a cutoff in Soviet aid to Cuba. Second, there had to be "market reforms." Gorbachev "has not moved off square one economically." Third, there had to be "democratic reforms." Since his return from Moscow, Nixon seemed less enthusiastic about Gorbachev's chances of survival, though he still saw no alternative to his rule. "The wave of the future is democratic reform not Communist reaction," Nixon wrote. Gorbachev "must establish his legitimacy by submitting his fate to a nationwide free election." Nixon concluded: "We should not delude ourselves into believing that aid would succeed without these far-reaching changes."

Neither Allison nor Yavlinsky was so deluded. Their plan was predicated on democratic reforms and a free market, and Western aid was conditioned on the achievement of both. Nixon's critique of their plan was unfair. Yet, during the process of thinking about the "grand bargain," Nixon seemed to have sharpened his own thinking about the emerging question of aiding Russia. Democratic and economic reform was clearly crucial as a precondition for Western aid, whether the concept was conceived by Nixon or Allison, but Nixon seemed to be leaning toward another requirement—that the leader of the Soviet Union also be freely elected. Gorbachev had moved the Soviet Union so dramatically toward democracy that Nixon began to toy with the notion that a Russian leader could have "legitimacy" only as a result of free elections.

On June 12, 1991, ten days after Nixon's op-ed piece appeared in the *Washington Post,* Yeltsin acquired the rich currency of political legitimacy by winning a popular, direct election as president of the Russian Republic, the largest component of the Soviet Union. He became the first freely elected leader in Russia's thousand-year history. Gorbachev remained the unelected president of the Soviet Union.

Nixon, like many other diplomatic observers, began to place his money on Yeltsin. Journalists, politicians, and scholars beat a path to Nixon's door seeking his counsel and insight. After all, he had recently met Yeltsin during a visit to Moscow. Among the scholars was Allison, who had been trying to talk to Nixon for several months. After Nixon's sharp critique, he tried even harder. At Blackwill's suggestion, Allison contacted Robert Ellsworth, a former U.S. ambassador to the North Atlantic Treaty Organization (NATO) in the Nixon administration. Ellsworth suggested that Allison write a letter to Nixon.

On July 9, 1991, Allison wrote, requesting a meeting. "I would like to seek your counsel on Western opportunities to shape the future in a manner consistent with our interests." Nixon agreed, and Allison flew to New Jersey on July 11, 1991. He spent two hours with Nixon, reviewing, among other things, the "grand bargain" and the state of U.S.–Soviet relations.

Why did Allison, a former dean of the Kennedy School, a professor at Harvard, a Democrat who had helped Michael Dukakis in 1988 and would later join the Clinton Pentagon, consider a meeting with Nixon so important that he would use every contact for the opportunity to confer with Nixon about Russia? Why was Nixon's approval so important to Allison? "If I'd caught him," Allison explained, "I'd have caught a whole lot." Meaning? "Nixon has a view that people in the Bush Administration take seriously. He's a credible spokesman for the right wing. He brings a political sense for the jugular that is quite stunning to me. He understands public policy better than most people."

Allison, a diligent note taker, dictated a memo to himself the morning after his meeting with Nixon. It showed that Nixon had changed his mind about the "grand bargain." No longer did he refer to it as a "grand con job," nor was he against a meaningful Western aid package. Now that Yeltsin had broken the ice and won a relatively free election, Nixon was ready to consider aid as part of a broad strategy to accelerate democratic and economic reform in Russia. Allison was surprised and pleased. Not only was Nixon "unfailingly gracious, sharp, engaged in the arguments, and thoughtful," but, according to the Allison memo, "we agree on more things than we disagree."

They agreed "to give history a nudge." Between them there was no disagreement about the "transcendent issue" of their time: the democratization of the Soviet Union. Not only was this seen as an honorable goal on its own merits, but, if achieved, it would satisfy the strategic national interests of the United States. There was, in Allison's words, "a fleeting moment of opportunity, where the configuration of economic facts and political forces in the Soviet Union are uniquely well-poised for engagement." But how could history be nudged?

Nixon told Allison one of his favorite stories. He said that it was the threat of Soviet expansionism that moved him and John Kennedy, one representing a conservative district and the other a liberal district, to support aid to Greece and Turkey in 1947. Without this threat, Nixon believed, there would have been no Marshall Plan, no Berlin airlift, no NATO, no program of foreign aid. Now that the Soviet economy was collapsing, Nixon seemed to be asking, what was the "threat" that would force the West to help Russia transform itself from a Communist dictatorship into a free market democracy? Production had fallen, Nixon estimated, 12 percent in 1990, and another 15 percent decline was envisaged for 1991. Such economic failure had foreshadowed Hitler's rise in Germany in the 1930s. Was there a Hitler in Russia's future in the 1990s? Nixon wondered, could that be the threat?

Nixon and Allison agreed that it was a matter of national— even international—importance to stimulate a vigorous debate on the shape and size of Western responsibility in molding the future course of Soviet development. But how was this to be done?

A month later, Yeltsin was atop the tank resisting the Moscow coup, and history turned a corner in Russia. Nixon felt that it beckoned to him to act.

4

BINGO!

Nineteen ninety-two provided Nixon with a perfect opportunity to try to change the foreign policy of his country. It was a presidential election year. George Bush, the Republican incumbent, had led a victorious allied coalition against Iraq the year before and seemed certain of reelection, even though the economy was sputtering and people felt uneasy. Yet, according to adviser Dimitri Simes, Nixon sensed a lack of leadership, a certain "void" in the policy debate. Where there should have been the fire of intellectual combat, there was instead a disconcerting sense of complacency, particularly in the Bush administration.

Nixon saw an urgent need for new policy initiatives. The old Soviet Union had just disintegrated into bewildered and competing countries. Simes, who had just returned from another trip to Moscow, told Nixon that he was especially concerned about Yeltsin's ability to build a democratic society in light of then Prime Minister Yegor Gaidar's plans to administer "shock therapy" to the faltering economy. Simes had visions (which Nixon shared) of mass unemployment, inflation, and hunger—of reactionaries in the Communist bureaucracy taking advantage of growing social and economic chaos to attempt another coup. In the chaos, though, Nixon saw not only danger but a golden opportunity for the West to affect the future of Russia and the world. Would Bush capitalize on the opportunity? In Nixon's view, no. The president seemed so smugly self-satisfied with his Persian Gulf triumph, so confident about his reelection, that Nixon felt he would not launch any new initiatives. He would not take any unnecessary risks.

Nixon was determined to sound the alarm. He saw himself as a modern-day Paul Revere, riding across the diplomatic landscape. As his former aide, William Gavin, put it, Nixon would become "larger than life," a figure above the political fray. Just as, in the early 1970s, he had launched an era of détente with the old Soviet Union, so twenty years later, encouraged by events in Russia and experts such as Allison and Simes, he would try to spark a nationwide debate about Western responsibility for the future of Russia.

Nixon believed that, for such a cause to be supported by both the administration and the American people, it would require an unmistakable threat to the nation, similar to the one posed by expansionist Communism in the late 1940s. Nixon also knew that every poll strongly indicated that the American people were infinitely more concerned about the sorry state of their own economy than about Russia's problems. Indeed, the very words "foreign" and "aid" generally drew a sullen hiss from his fellow Republicans in Congress. At this moment what was needed from the White House, Nixon felt, was boldness, audacity, vision, but what the country was getting was caution and timidity.

How was he to ignite a debate about Russia?

Nixon was, as always, resourceful. It was January, and he had just finished another book, *Seize the Moment*, his latest formula for reasserting American leadership of a chaotic world. His publisher, with his approval, had arranged a number of promotional interviews on television, and he could use them to sell his evolving ideas about helping Russia. He was also preparing a high-profile conference in Washington, which he saw as a forum for discussing the radically changed situation in the world. Better than most politicians approaching the age of eighty, he appreciated the importance of such a forum for generating news. In an age of image and television, of the soundbite, and of the well-timed and orchestrated leak, Nixon was the master spin-merchant—and he knew it. He had a story, and he intended to sell it.

Planning for the conference had been under way for many months. According to Simes, shortly after Nixon's March–April 1991 visit to Moscow, Simes had proposed in general terms that the Nixon Library sponsor a Washington conference on world events. Simes told me that the conference was not intended to be used as a vehicle for the "rehabilitation of Richard Nixon." It had to stand "on its own merits." Simes envisaged the conference as a first step toward the establishment of a Nixon foreign policy institute, probably in Washington. The conference would be arranged to play to Nixon's strengths in foreign policy. Simes assured Nixon that he, Simes, would assume responsibility for organizing the conference, that John Taylor would do the fund raising, and that Nixon would not be bothered with any of the details.

The selection of a chairperson for the conference proved to be an interesting exercise. Henry Kissinger would have been the obvious choice. After all, he had been Nixon's national security adviser and Secretary of State. But in recent years relations between the two men had become so strained that Simes decided instead to ask one of his Carnegie colleagues, James Schlesinger, who had served as Nixon's last Secretary of Defense.

Even this selection, though, posed a potential problem. Toward the end of the Nixon presidency, Nixon and Schlesinger had clashed over the terms of an arms control proposal, Schlesinger urging a much tougher line than Nixon. Nixon was furious. He felt that if it had not been for the debilitating effect of Watergate,

Schlesinger would never have had the guts to challenge his judgment. And, in the final days, Schlesinger ordered the Joint Chiefs of Staff to advise him of any White House order to use military force to protect the president from impeachment, so concerned was the Secretary of Defense that Nixon had become unhinged. Still, Nixon chose to ignore their previous history, and Schlesinger accepted the assignment.

"I owe a fair amount to Mr. Nixon," Schlesinger recalled one day. "So long as he doesn't ask me to do anything illegal or unethical, I'm pleased and honored to help him. We should not forget: Nixon made great contributions to the country's foreign policy. He's our most skilled leader since Eisenhower."

George Shultz and William Simon, two other members of the Nixon Cabinet, were also asked to be members of the conference's steering committee, but they contributed little more than their names.

Simes met with Nixon in the fall of 1991 to review plans for the conference. Nixon disapproved of the tentative title—"The New World Order." For one thing, it sounded too derivatively drawn from Bush's own vision of the post–Gulf War world. For another, Nixon was concerned that his former speechwriter, Pat Buchanan, who was about to challenge Bush with a decidedly isolationist message, would rip into the conference for sounding too internationalist. Nixon changed the title first to "The New International Environment: America's Role in the Emerging World" and eventually to just "America's Role in the Emerging World."

As usual, Nixon had his own agenda. Simes had always felt that the conference should be serious, edging toward scholarly, a broad review of the world in the aftermath of the Cold War. Nixon allowed Simes to believe that the conference would in fact develop along these lines, but from the beginning it was clear that Nixon had always intended to transform Simes's vision, no matter how it was officially framed, into a more tightly focused discussion about Russia.

Simes and Schlesinger worked diligently to organize the conference. Hundreds of politicians, officials, diplomats, scholars, and journalists were invited. It was to feature a star-studded cast, including such luminaries as Kissinger, CIA Director Robert Gates, trade negotiator Carla Hills, Senators Daniel Patrick Moynihan and Warren Rudman, and Russian Ambassador Vladimir P. Lukin.

The main ballroom of the Four Seasons Hotel was booked for March 11–12, 1992. Papers were commissioned for panels on Asia, the Middle East, and Europe. Simes told me, "Not a single person turned us down." Scholars were flattered to be invited. Both Simes and Schlesinger operated on a single guiding principle: the conference was to be nonpartisan, meaning that even someone like Robert Reich of Harvard's Kennedy School of Government, an adviser to Bill Clinton who would later become his Secretary of Labor, could be invited to speak, and that no participants were to be excluded because of old differences with Nixon. "Enemies lists" would not be allowed to determine the guest list. (Even I got an invitation, but I could not attend because I had already accepted an earlier invitation to another conference.) It was to be a platform for a serious discussion of world affairs; in Schlesinger's words, "It was to be a highly respected exercise."

Simes and Schlesinger arranged the schedule so that Nixon would speak at lunch, and Bush at a black tie dinner. At least that was their hope. From earlier discussions, they knew that Nixon felt strongly that the presence of the president would underscore a U.S. determination to remain committed to its global responsibilities, in spite of a widespread perception from campaign rhetoric that the United States was withdrawing from the world now that the Cold War was over. Bush's presence would also represent another step toward Nixon's ultimate rehabilitation, but this aim was left unspoken.

Question: who was to invite the president? Simes and Schlesinger felt that Nixon ought to send him a letter of invitation, but Nixon rejected the idea. According to Simes, Nixon thought it might be seen as "presumptuous." So Schlesinger assumed the responsibility of inviting the president in a letter to Brent Scowcroft, the national security adviser, and Simes reinforced the invitation in letters to both Scowcroft and Edward Hewett, a Soviet specialist on the National Security Council (NSC) staff. Weeks passed without any definitive word from the White House, which was becoming increasingly absorbed with the Buchanan challenge. How was Nixon to read the silence? Taylor suggested that Julie Nixon Eisenhower write a personal letter of invitation to the president, but Nixon vetoed the idea. In early February, with the conference only a little more than a month away, Simes faxed a special appeal to Nixon, urging him to let his daughter send the letter. She was, after all, chairperson of the steering committee. Nixon finally gave his approval.

Part of the reason for the silence might well have been the old strains in the Bush-Nixon relationship. Bush and Nixon came from two worlds and two wings of the Republican Party. Nixon was the poor, hard-working politician who had made it, rising to the presidency on the strength of ambition, determination, and ruthlessness. Bush had emerged from what Garry Wills called "the evanescing party of his father—the Wall Street internationalist party of paternalistic 'Wise Men'" (Wills, *New York Review of Books,* August 13, 1992, p. 21). Nixon both loathed and envied Bush, often joking bitterly with aides that the Yale-educated New Englander had been "born with a silver spoon in his mouth." Just as Lyndon Johnson resented John Kennedy's style and education, so, too, did Nixon resent Bush's wealth and status. For his part, Bush knew what Nixon thought of him, but, an associate said, he "suffered in silence," feeling "a strange loyalty, a deep gratitude, to Nixon" (Wills, ibid.).

They had met for the first time in 1952, when Bush organized a reception in Midland, Texas, for Nixon, then the visiting vice-presidential candidate. Years later, even though Bush's father, former Senator Prescott Bush of Connecticut, had spoken out against the deepening U.S. involvement in Vietnam, Bush supported Nixon and the war. In 1970, when Nixon, as president, urged Bush to run for the Senate, Bush ran, rejecting his father's advice that he hold on to his safe House seat. According to Wills, Nixon promised "every form of help," even dangling the possibility of a major Cabinet position or even the vice-presidency in 1972 if Bush were to lose. He lost to conservative Democrat Lloyd Bentsen. As compensation, Nixon offered Bush the job of U.N. ambassador after a number of other prospects, including Daniel Patrick Moynihan, had turned it down. Why had Bush listened to the White House and not his father? His campaign manager, Marvin Collins, explained that Bush was trying to appear strong: "Haldeman and those guys in the White House were calling Bush weak, saying he had no balls, he wouldn't stand up to people" (Wills, ibid., p. 25).

After the 1972 election, which Nixon won in a landslide despite stories alleging his complicity in the Watergate break-in, George Shultz, then Secretary of the Treasury, offered Bush a major job in a revamped executive branch, but before Bush could say yes, Nixon said no, offering Bush instead the rather thankless post of chairman of the Republican National Committee in the midst of a spreading political scandal. Reluctantly, Bush accepted the post, and it was then left to him to assert Nixon's innocence in the face of mounting evidence that the president was guilty of obstructing justice. Among Nixon's dwindling band of supporters at that time, Bush was regarded as "a weakling, a wimp." In private, in the spring of 1973, Bush pleaded for "some action that would get us off the defensive," and, on August 7, 1974, a few days before Nixon's resignation, Bush suggested to the president in a private letter that he resign for the good of the country. To Nixon, this was an example of "candy ass" treachery (Wills, ibid., p. 26).

Nixon's negative attitude toward Bush persisted even after Reagan had selected Bush as his vice-presidential running mate. In 1983, a year before Reagan's landslide victory over Walter Mondale, Nixon appeared on CNN's "Crossfire" with co-host Pat Buchanan and strongly suggested that Vice-President Bush ought to be dumped from the GOP ticket.[1] Nixon told Buchanan that Bush was "not good on the attack" and Reagan needed someone "stronger." Reagan should "look over the team and strengthen it." Why? Because, Nixon projected, this was going to be "one of the roughest, dirtiest campaigns in history . . . a rough bloody battle." It was, in fact, "rough" and "bloody" on occasion, principally because of GOP attacks against Mondale's position on raising taxes, but Reagan could have won it with Mickey Mouse as a running mate.

In 1988, during the presidential primaries, Nixon continued to underestimate Bush's skills as a tough campaigner. In a memo he privately circulated to friends, he described Bush as "a weak individual on television" and Senator Dole, his principal opponent, as "strong and courageous." In February 1988, Bush went on the offensive on television and denounced and distorted Dole's tax

1. "Crossfire" had two hosts. In typical CNN fashion, one was a conservative, the other was a liberal. Paired with Buchanan was Tom Braden, who took liberal stands on most issues. Nixon refused to be interviewed by Braden, expressing a preference for his friend Buchanan. CNN, then a vulnerable upstart in the news business, yielded to Nixon's demand. Braden withdrew.

policy—and won the crucial New Hampshire primary, opening the way for his nomination and election as president.

Four years later, Nixon wanted a presidential seal of approval for his Washington conference, despite his less than consistent support for Bush. In other words, he needed Bush a lot more than Bush needed him. A more cautious politician would have kept a low profile, encouraging his aides to make discreet inquiries at the White House about whether the president would speak on March 11. But Nixon was a gambler. His views about Russia had evolved to the point where he felt Western action was urgent. Even though he had not yet heard whether Bush would attend his conference, Nixon decided to roll the dice—specifically, to launch a public relations campaign aimed at pressuring the Bush administration and Congress to consider an unpopular cause in the midst of a presidential race, namely, a major aid program for Russia. The campaign included television interviews, op-ed pieces, magazine articles, telephone calls, intimate lunches and dinners—and a memo critical of the president that Nixon was thinking of writing and circulating with a view to stirring the pot.

Television was on the top of Nixon's list. It served two purposes: selling his new book and honing his new message. His first appearances were on ABC's "Nightline" on January 7, 1992, and CNN's "Larry King Live" on January 8, 1992.

"Nightline" anchor Ted Koppel had been trying to get Nixon to appear in a documentary for several years. On one occasion, Koppel and ABC News president Roone Arledge had proposed a special program that would have had Koppel accompany Nixon to the scenes of his greatest triumphs—Beijing, Moscow, Caracas—and there have Nixon reminisce about his experiences. Koppel said that they would also have gone to Watergate, the scene of his great failure. Nixon was close to accepting the proposal but at the last minute declined, saying that he had promised his wife that he would never again appear on ABC television after the network had run a movie adaptation of the Woodward-Bernstein book, *The Final Days,* several years before.

In November 1991, Koppel resumed his efforts to interview Nixon. He visited the former president in his New Jersey office and offered to do a special one-hour edition of his program if Nixon promised that "Nightline" would be his first TV appearance on the book tour. It was a deal. "We realized that the best way to get Nixon was to tie his appearance to his book," said Koppel. "Nixon had given me a typewritten manuscript of his book. I read it and wanted to ask him questions about the book and other things. . . . Interviewing Nixon is one of the most fascinating political experiences."

In the course of the interview, which focused primarily on foreign affairs, Nixon said that he "wrote off" Gorbachev in September 1991, a month after the failed coup. He did not think Yeltsin was "the second coming," but he did think Yeltsin had "the power" to run Russia. "He is for the free market, he is going to adopt a foreign policy which is not aggressive. . . . Anybody who does these things deserves the support of the United States. We should hope that he survives." Nixon then carefully approached the subject of an American aid program for Russia. He said, "The U.S. has to be helpful . . . for the transition" from the old Communist system to a new democratic system, but, because dollars were scarce in the United States, he stressed that Germany and Japan "should pick up a lot of the tab." He left the implication that the United States would pick up the rest. "As far as foreign aid is concerned," he told Koppel, "we're doing it for our own interests," but he did not define the interests, nor the threat that he saw in the shadows of the new Russia.

Speaking with Larry King on the evening before his seventy-ninth birthday, Nixon said that he was "pretty good at predicting elections and fairly good at predicting foreign policy," but, referring to the August coup attempt, "I would not have predicted it would have happened." Could the new Russian revolution succeed? "It's a close call," Nixon responded. "But it is the best bet that we have, because Yeltsin has a very good group of people around him. He has done what Gorbachev would not do. He has adopted the free market policies, and he is going to try to unleash the creative abilities of the Russian people."

Then in the following exchange rose the faint outline of the threat that Nixon was later to define in more alarming terms:

NIXON: "Yeltsin must not fail, because if he fails, it means that not the Communists will come back, but an authoritarian old guard will come back."

KING: "So we must help?"

NIXON: "We must help, without question."

KING: "Financially?"

NIXON: "We must help financially.... The rest of Europe, Japan and the rest must assume the primary burden for providing the transitional funds, the humanitarian aid that Russia and the Soviet Union needs at this time. The U.S. cannot do it alone. We should simply provide, however, the leadership."

Later in the broadcast, Nixon offered more detail. "We're moving into uncharted waters. We don't know what's going to happen in Russia after just one year, for example—or less than a year of a democratic government there."

What emerged from these interviews was that Nixon had thrown his support unmistakably to Yeltsin and to the idea of American financial aid to Russia, but he was still groping for a definition of the elusive "threat" that would galvanize the president and Congress into action.

Nixon then took his message to *Time* magazine. "He usually comes to us when he has a piece to propose," said Richard Duncan, an executive editor at *Time*. A Nixon aide called Strobe Talbott, who once told me, "I'm his case officer at *Time*." Would the magazine be interested in an RN offering? About what? U.S. policy toward Russia. Talbott liked the idea, but before giving his formal approval, he checked with Duncan, and Duncan checked with editor Henry Muller. "We'd love to see it," Duncan said. There was no obligation on *Time*'s part to publish the Nixon column, but *Time* had never turned down the former president.

Space at *Time* is a precious commodity. *Time* publishes a column a week. Forty or so a year are commissioned from *Time*'s regular columnists, meaning there is room for only a dozen other columns. Hundreds of offerings arrive "over the transom," many of them, according to Duncan, "modeled on op-ed pieces that you'd normally see in the *Times*." These are rejected. *Time* wants "a more formal essay," a carefully drafted piece on a large theme.

So the idea of Nixon doing a column about Russia was instantly appealing to *Time*'s editors. "Coming from him," Duncan said, "we thought it would be significant and thoughtful." *Time*, in its April 2, 1990, issue, had run Nixon on its cover and published long excerpts from his memoir, *In the Arena*. Nixon, as a former president, represented both stature and, in his case, controversy—surefire ingredients in the supercharged competition among American magazines. He was also perceived as a recognized guru on foreign policy, a Cold Warrior who had turned a corner. "It's an interesting experience editing him," said Talbott. "He's easy to work with. He turned in very solid pieces of work, and he didn't yell and scream about cuts." Duncan told me, "Actually, it wasn't a bad piece—an essay with a strong linear argument." Ronald Kriss, another editor, summed up the magazine's view: "It was current, worthy, and we ran it."

The Nixon column appeared on page 27 of the January 13, 1992, issue of *Time*. "Now is the time to provide economic aid," it began, "to pro-reform Republics of the new Commonwealth of Independent States," which had been formed a month before. They "deserve our help," he wrote, and Yeltsin "must not fail." Why help? Because, Nixon continued, "no better alternative exists," and "the reform of Russia is a key to the reform of the other Republics." But in this piece, Nixon did not directly criticize the administration, limiting his criticism time and again to the vague political and diplomatic composite known as "the West," which he said has been "slow" to recognize the opportunity and come to Russia's aid.

He then listed four policy recommendations:

1. "Create a U.S.-led organization to spearhead Western aid efforts."
2. "Provide accelerated assistance to agricultural sectors."
3. "Establish 'enterprise funds' for reformist Republics."
4. "Expand educational and information-exchange programs."

Though these were, for their time, interesting and important recommendations, the Nixon column attracted very little attention. At the daily White House and State Department briefings, no reporter asked a question about it, and the spokespersons volunteered no administration response. Disappointed, the former president then put his mind to the memo, still not certain how he would sharpen his focus and draw blood.

Inspiration came from two unexpected sources: the new Russian leadership and a Washington columnist.

On January 30, 1992, Yeltsin flew into New York for a special summit meeting of the U.N. Security Council, the first time that "Russia" formally replaced the "Soviet Union" on the international stage. Emblazoned on the fuselage of his giant IL-62 jet was the single word "RUSSIA." From New York, Yeltsin was to fly to Camp David for an informal meeting with Bush. During a refueling stop in London, Yeltsin struck conciliatory themes: democracy and a free market in Russia, Western credit and capital, nuclear disarmament. He urged Britain, France, and China to join the United States and Russia in cutting their nuclear arsenals. He promised to "retarget" Russia's ICBMs aimed at Europe and the United States, a pledge the BBC quickly put on the air as a bulletin: "Russian Missiles No Longer Aimed at British Cities."

Yeltsin's high-visibility debut at the United Nations coincided with a substantial revamping of administration policy toward the Russian president. Less than two months before, in early December, senior U.S. officials were still openly disdainful of Yeltsin, recalling that during his first visit to the United States in September 1989 he had been described in newspaper stories as a drunkard and a buffoon. Even in mid-January, when the administration hosted an international gathering in Washington to discuss the issue of aid to Russia, officials were so uncertain about Yeltsin's staying power, not to mention his mental stability, that they decided to put some deliberate distance between the Bush and Yeltsin administrations. But now the U.S. attitude changed, partly as a result of smart diplomacy and press relations in Moscow.

Some of Yeltsin's closest advisers made a point of cultivating Robert Strauss, who was then U.S. ambassador to Moscow. Though Strauss, a Democrat, was an accomplished pro at the game of American politics, he was only a shrewd innocent about Russian politics; he did not speak Russian, and his knowledge of Russian history and literature was limited. He was briefed time and again by Russian officials about the revolutionary changes they were trying to initiate—a timetable for democracy and a market economy. They stressed that Yeltsin's commitment to radical reform was fixed and firm. And always there was an implied warning: that if Yeltsin somehow failed, his successor would almost certainly be a right wing autocrat. As one official put it, "The only alternative to Yeltsin is Stalin—an authoritarian regime."

Though the line was obviously self-serving, it coincided with Strauss's own vision of Russia's immediate future. In cable after cable to the State Department, he pleaded for understanding, sympathy, and, most important, a warm welcome for Yeltsin at Camp David and a public commitment to help him transform Russia. From both Strauss in his cables and the American press in their dispatches from Moscow, this drumbeat of analysis was heard and read. It ultimately led a rather reluctant administration to adjust its Russia policy, not yet to the point of writing a blank check but certainly to the point of recrafting official rhetoric and warming the atmosphere. In any case, Yeltsin was coming to the United Nations, and there was no longer time for political procrastination, even in the midst of a presidential campaign.

No sooner had the man from Moscow, only recently scorned as a country bumpkin, reached New York than he began to dominate press coverage. He was the lead story in the *New York Times,* the *Los Angeles Times,* and the *Washington Post.* Network coverage was extensive. Reporters were briefed constantly by American and Russian spokespersons. The new upbeat melody of U.S.–Russian relations could now be heard everywhere. At a private dinner for Yeltsin, hosted by the Federal Reserve Bank of New York, to which eighty executives from business, government, and banking were invited, the Russian leader was hailed as the first democratically elected president in his country's history. He in

turn described Russia, according to then Foreign Ministry spokesman Vitaly Churkin, as "a new phenomenon in international life.
There has been a qualitative change. Now that we're regarded as
fully part of the democratic world, we would like to build our
relations with other countries belonging to that world as friends
and maybe as allies" (*New York Times,* February 1, 1992, p. 5).
(Simes told me that he had arranged for a fifteen-minute private
meeting between Nixon and Yeltsin immediately after the dinner,
but Nixon declined, saying, "This is George's show.")

Yeltsin's belief was that, as the leader of a great country, he
should not be the one asking for a Western handout. In all of his
meetings, he decided, he would simply describe the problem, state
Russia's needs, warn of calamity if his reform program failed, and
then hope that the aid would be forthcoming.

At Camp David, the rhetoric was friendly, and the atmosphere
warm. The two presidents were quickly on a first-name basis.
George drove Boris around in a golf cart, presented him with a
fur-lined White House parka and a pair of hand-tooled Texas
cowboy boots, and then proclaimed that a "new era" in U.S.–
Russian relations had begun. But there was no commitment of
aid, and Yeltsin left disappointed. "We've been talking about this
[Western fund to stabilize the ruble] for seven months and unfortunately, so far, nothing has been done," he told reporters before
returning to Moscow. "And that's dangerous. Today Russia is facing the last opportunity to defend democracy. . . . We are calling
for cooperation for the whole world, because if the reform in Russia goes under, that means there will be a Cold War. The Cold
War will turn into a 'hot war' and another arms race."

This was clearly the Russian "line," and it was well orchestrated.
In briefings with reporters, Dmitri Volkogonov, a close adviser to
Yeltsin and a renowned military historian who was then exploring

the darkest secrets of the Stalin archives, echoed Yeltsin's warning: "If the West does not help us with reforms, there might be a reversal . . . [that would] turn the world back to confrontation."

Prime Minister Gaidar, who was also in the Yeltsin entourage, raised a rather important question. "Where do the West's interests lie?" He answered his own question. "Certainly not in a return to past oppression, certainly not in the re-establishment of an ideologically aggressive political and economic system, certainly not in another battle for world supremacy. But still the West hesitates."

Someone identified by reporter Michael Parks of the *Los Angeles Times* as a "senior Russian official accompanying Yeltsin" asked the question that would soon catapult a Nixon memo into a direct political challenge to the president: "Who lost Russia?" With a relevance that seemed specially crafted for the undercurrents of American politics, the "senior Russian official" said: "That could very well be the question historians will put to President Bush if our reforms fail through lack of support. The basic task, of course, rests with us, but Bush and the West must play an essential role in supporting the change. That takes money, but more than just plain dollars, it takes political courage and farsightedness."[2]

"Who lost Russia?"—the question first attributed in a February 3, 1992, newspaper story to a "senior Russian official"—

2. I am guessing by the way Parks wrote his story that his source was Gaidar but that Gaidar did not want to be quoted. A reporter prefers to name a source, to put the information "on the record." But a source does not always wish to be identified, in which case the information is treated as "background," meaning it can be used, even with quotes, but the source is not to be identified by name, only by organization or government, as in "U.S. officials said today" or "according to a senior Russian official accompanying Yeltsin." Beyond "background," there is "deep background," which means that neither the source's name nor his country or organization can be identified, and the reporter is left in the uncomfortable position of either using the information without any direct attribution, producing such awkward phraseology as "Yeltsin is said to believe" or "It has come to light here that," or not using it at all.

popped up again as the lead of a syndicated column by Charles Krauthammer that appeared in the *Washington Post* (and many other newspapers) on February 14, 1992. "Who lost Russia?" Krauthammer asked. "If Yeltsin falls, the question will be asked. So we might as well ask it now. Preemptive scapegoating might do some good, because, for the moment, the President's men seem serenely indifferent to Yeltsin's prospects in Moscow. They are far more concerned about Bush's prospects in New Hampshire. And, spooked by Pat Buchanan's isolationism, they see nothing but political risk in raising the issue of Russian aid."

Krauthammer continued: "If Yeltsin does fall, and is replaced by an authoritarian anti-Western regime, there will be a reckoning. Not the McCarthyite witch hunts that fed on the Who Lost China? hysteria of the 1950's, but blame and opprobrium enough. To blunder away the most favorable foreign development of this half-century would, for an administration that prides itself on its foreign policy stewardship, be a devastating blow."

Two weeks later, Nixon acknowledged that he owed Krauthammer a debt. In a brief note that he sent to Krauthammer, attached to a copy of the controversial memo, Nixon wrote, "This memo was inspired by your piece." Nixon never acknowledged his debt in public, only in this private note, clearly intended to flatter the columnist. Krauthammer never raised an objection. Why, one of his admirers asked, would he want "to get into a pissing match with Nixon"? Krauthammer may also have recognized that it is in the nature of the columnist's craft to spark ideas, not necessarily to be credited with the spark. It occurred to me at the time that Walter Lippmann, in a 1946 series in the *New York Herald Tribune* and later in a book, was the first writer to come up with the historic phrase "Cold War," but who remembered his authorship?

Bingo! All along Nixon had been waiting for the "threat," the one dramatic, inescapable question or formula that not only would capture the president's attention but also would engage his—and the nation's—deepest fears. "Who lost Russia?" Within a matter of days after Yeltsin's return to Moscow and the publication of the Krauthammer column, Nixon began to write the memo that triggered a train of events that would change the campaign debate about foreign policy in the spring of 1992.

5

"WHO LOST RUSSIA?"

"The conference was my idea," Simes said, without hesitation. "The memo was Nixon's. He deserves all the credit. It's his—and his alone."

In the past, Nixon would, on occasion, write a book or a memo on a controversial subject and privately circulate it among former aides, friends, and journalists. In 1983 he wrote, published, and distributed 115 copies of his book *Real Peace,* and in 1988 he circulated a candid memo handicapping the Republican field of presidential candidates. On both occasions, he found that this unorthodox approach generated a rush of attention and admiration. He was not only informing people; he was also reminding them of his continuing involvement in public policy. This time, by directing the question of "Who lost Russia?" at President Bush, Nixon knew that he was throwing a live hand grenade at the White House. The memo would surely leak and explode on the front page and on the evening news. That was his intention.

In preparing this memo, Nixon was assisted by researcher Monica Crowley, a Colgate graduate with a degree in Russian studies, and Marin Strmecki, a Harvard graduate who helped, as he put it, "facilitate" a number of Nixon book projects during the 1980s and who later, in the waning months of the Bush administration, joined the Policy Planning Staff of the Pentagon. Nixon dictated the first draft of the memo into a small tape recorder.

Strmecki reworked the draft, making it seem "more written than spoken." Nixon then wrote a second and a third draft of what turned out to be slightly more than four pages of tightly reasoned, single-spaced criticism of the Bush administration's policy toward Russia. "It's quintessentially RN," said Strmecki proudly. "He wanted to speak out in very forceful terms, and he did" (interview, August 29, 1992).

Nixon outlined his stark vision of a world balanced precariously between a new era of democracy in a Russia led by Boris Yeltsin and a desperate descent into global chaos produced by a "dangerous new despotism" in the Kremlin. Writing more as a polemicist than as a statesman, Nixon framed the argument in extreme terms—international bliss with Yeltsin or international hell without him. Subtlety was not in his brief.

It is worth quoting extensively from the Nixon memo to understand the historical and political context in which his proposals were advanced and to appreciate his capacity for spotting, squeezing, and, if necessary, cutting the jugular.

Nixon immediately zeroed in on what he regarded as the central shortcoming of the primary season. "While the candidates have addressed scores of significant issues in the presidential campaign," he began, "the most important issue since the end of World War II—the fate of the political and economic reforms in Russia—has been virtually ignored. As a result, the United States and the West risk snatching defeat in the cold war from the jaws of victory." In his *Time* magazine column, Nixon had directed his criticism at the "West"; now he was specifically targeting the United States.

"Today the ideas of freedom are on trial. If they fail to produce a better life in Russia and the other former Soviet republics, a new and more dangerous despotism will take power, with the people trading freedom for security and entrusting their future to old hands with new faces.

"We are at a watershed moment in history. The historical significance of the democratic revolution in the Soviet Union compares only with events like the defeat of Napoleon at Waterloo in 1815, the Versailles Peace Conference in 1918, and the creation of NATO and the Marshall Plan in 1948. . . . While opportunities and dangers on that same order of magnitude face us today, the West has failed so far to seize the moment to shape the history of the next half century." Nixon was forever the activist, ready to "seize" the opportunities in the East rather than circle them cautiously, as the Bush administration seemed to be doing.

"Russia is the key to success. It is there that the final battle of the cold war will be won or lost. The stakes could not be higher. If freedom succeeds in Russia—if President Yeltsin's economic reforms succeed in creating a successful free-market economy—the future will hold the promise of reduced spending on arms, cooperation in coping with crises around the world, and economic growth through expanded international trade. . . .

"If Yeltsin fails, the prospects for the next fifty years will turn grim. The Russian people will not turn back to Communism. But a new, more dangerous despotism based on extremist Russian nationalism will take power. . . . The leaders of a new despotism, who have already been organizing themselves to take over in the event that Yeltsin's reforms fail, will stoke nationalist passions and exploit the tendency of the Russian people to turn to the strong hand—even to dictatorship—during times of trouble."

The "threat" was now beginning to materialize in the Nixon memo. He framed it in a worst case scenario.

"If a new despotism prevails, everything gained in the great peaceful revolution of 1991 will be lost." Everything? "War could break out in the former Soviet Union as the new despots use force to restore the 'historical borders' of Russia. The new East European democracies would be imperiled. China's totalitarians would breathe a sigh of relief. The new Russian regime—whose leaders would cozy up to the Soviet Union's former clients in Iraq, Syria, Libya, and North Korea—would threaten our interests in hot spots around the world. It would sell conventional weapons, ballistic missiles, and nuclear technology to any buyer. A new Russian despotism inspired by imperial nationalism shorn of the baggage of the dying faith of Communism would be even more dangerous than Soviet totalitarianism."

Nixon was deliberately overstating the threat to strengthen his case. But at this point a serious question arises: Why would a new Russian despotism be any more dangerous to American interests than the old Soviet totalitarianism? It would seem to be quite the other way around. The Soviet military establishment, once an effective force, had been badly set back in recent years. The East European empire had been shattered. Communist Party influence and ideology around the world, undermining Western interests, had been substantially reduced. The Russian economy had been thrown into absolute turmoil, with state enterprises largely destroyed. No matter which brand of authoritarianism ruled in Moscow, the new leaders, wearing black, brown, or red shirts, would be absorbed primarily with feeding an unhappy and rebellious people and securing their borders.

Having constructed the threat, Nixon now veered in what was for him an unusual direction. He had always believed that nations were moved by "interests" rather than "personalities," yet here he was laying out the reasons why the West had to help not Russia but Yeltsin. "In light of the stakes involved, the West must do everything it can to help President Yeltsin succeed. Yeltsin has been maligned by friends of freedom in the West who should have known better." Did Nixon mean President Bush, Secretary of State Baker, and others who had until recently considered Yeltsin a joke? "Some say that he is not democratic enough politically, others that he is not smart enough intellectually, and still others that he is not smooth enough socially. A few who dismissed him as a boob in the past now seem to be hoping for his failure so that they can claim to have been proved right. That thinking is not worthy of the world's only superpower.

"Like all strong leaders who try to make a difference, Yeltsin is not perfect. He has made serious mistakes. But he is an extraordinary historic figure. He is the first Russian leader in history chosen through free elections. Unlike Gorbachev, he has irrevocably repudiated socialism as well as Communism. He risked his life in facing down a gang of card-carrying killers in the coup attempt in August, 1991." Card-carrying? A moment of dark nostalgia for the early 1950s? "He has moved decisively toward privatization of Soviet enterprises and decollectivization of Soviet agriculture, steps Gorbachev refused even to consider. He has completely cut off the $15 billion in foreign aid and trade subsidies that Gorbachev in his 1990 budget continued to provide to Cuba and other anti-American Communist losers in the developing world. He has not only matched but exceeded the cuts in nuclear weapons proposed by President Bush." In his first direct reference to the president, Nixon seemed to be criticizing him for being too timid in his proposed cuts in nuclear weapons. He concluded his thought: "The bottom line is that Yeltsin is the most pro-Western leader of Russia in history. Moreover, whatever his flaws, the alternative of a new despotism would be infinitely worse."

For purposes of argument, Nixon presented his case in terms of two clearcut alternatives: Yeltsin and democracy on the one side, and a new despotism worse than the old Soviet totalitarianism on the other. But why must there be only two possibilities—

and these two possibilities? In a revolution of such rich unpredict-
ability and in a country whose history has known such violent
swings of mood and direction, why could there not be five or
ten other possibilities, ranging from a Jeffersonian democracy to
a Swedish form of socialism to a fascist dictatorship?

In his analysis Nixon then raised the first of a number of key
questions. "What has [sic] the United States and the West done so
far to help Russia's first democratic, free-market oriented, non-
expansionist government? We have provided credits for the purchase of agricultural products. We have held a photo-opportunity
international conference of fifty-seven foreign secretaries that was
long on rhetoric but short on action." Nixon's disdain for Baker,
who had presided over this conference, was emerging more
clearly. "We are sending sixty cargo-planes of surplus food and
medical supplies left over from the Persian Gulf war. We have
decided to send 200 Peace Corps volunteers—a generous action
if the target of our aid were a small country like Upper Volta but
mere tokenism if applied to Russia, a nation of almost 200 million
people covering one-seventh of the world's land mass." Barely dis-
guising his contempt, Nixon strung out this laundry list of administration actions, which he knew would sound ridiculous, in order
to set up this devastating judgment: "This is a pathetically inadequate response in light of the opportunities and dangers we face
in the crisis in the former Soviet Union." Nixon knew the journalistic craft well enough to be certain that he had just written the
headline for many news stories: Nixon blasts Bush.

Another question, oddly reminiscent of one of Lenin's most
famous pamphlets: "What is to be done?" Nixon asked. His answer: "To meet the moment, the West must step up to the task of
helping President Yeltsin's government in six crucial ways:"

Here Nixon elaborated on the points he had originally written
for *Time,* changing the thrust of only one of them:

—"We must provide humanitarian food and medical aid to get Russia through the critical months until Yeltsin's reforms have a chance to start working.

—"We must create a 'free enterprise corps' that will send thousands of Western managers to Russia to infuse newly independent enterprises with free market know-how.

—"We must reschedule Soviet debt incurred during the Gorbachev era and defer interest payments until the new market economy begins to function.

—"We must allow greater access to Western markets for Russia's exports.

—"We must be ready to join with others to provide tens of billions of dollars for currency stabilization through the IMF or other means as soon as Russia reins in the growth of its money supply.

—"We must create a single Western-led organization to assess Soviet needs and coordinate wide-ranging governmental and private aid projects, as the United States did when embarking on the rebuilding of Western Europe after World War II." In his *Time* magazine article, Nixon had proposed that this organization be led by the United States. Now he widened the responsibility to embrace all of the West.

Even if the administration had planned to offer some help to Russia, Nixon criticized the timetable. "In light of the depth of the Russian economic crisis, there is no time to lose. Those who would put off major action on these fronts until the next international aid conference in July 1992 could find that this is too little and too late." Nixon's assessment of Bush's plans was accurate. This was precisely what the president had intended to do.

Still another question, as Nixon escalated the pressure on the president: "Can we afford these initiatives?" His answer: "As Herb

Stein has pointed out, 'the United States is a very rich nation. We are not rich enough to do everything, but we are rich enough to do everything important.' . . . The United States as the strongest and richest nation in the world must provide the leadership."

Now Nixon reached for a gambling metaphor. "We must be willing to bear our share of the burden. To play in this game, we must have a seat at the table. To get a seat at the table, we must be ready to put some chips in the pot. The stakes are high, and we are playing as if it were a penny ante game."

Nixon then pulled out all the stops. He questioned Bush's capacity for bold leadership and raised *the question.* "It is a tough call politically. Opinion polls indicate that foreign policy rates only in the single digits among issues that voters consider to be important. The American people overwhelmingly oppose all foreign aid because they want to see that money spent on solving our problems at home. But the mark of great political leadership is not simply to support what is popular but to make what is unpopular popular if that serves America's national interest. In addition, what seems politically profitable in the short run may prove costly in the long run. The hot-button issue in the 1950s was, 'Who lost China?' If Yeltsin goes down, the question of 'Who lost Russia?' will be an infinitely more devastating issue in the 1990s."

The politician who more than any other in the early 1950s exploited the "Red China" scare was now urging one of his successors to avoid the pitfalls of an "infinitely more devastating" scare in the 1990s. Nixon was, in effect, telling Bush that if he didn't follow the Nixon formula, and if Yeltsin collapsed and a new despotism emerged, Bush would be saddled with the political responsibility. Right or wrong, he would be seen as the president who "lost" Russia. This was an example, *New York Times* columnist William Safire told me, of Nixon thinking not as "another, off-the-rack foreign policy specialist" but as an "imaginative, hard-nosed" politician, who intended to force the President to act—and the sooner the better.

Others might have seen it as an example of a thoroughly un-principled politician pushing a new hot-button of fear to pressure Bush to follow his policy on aid to Russia. "Who lost China?" had become "Who lost Russia?"

Nixon then linked aid to Russia to the budget deficit. "Those who oppose aid argue that charity begins at home. I agree. But aid to Russia and other reformist republics of the former Soviet Union is not charity. We must recognize that what helps us abroad helps us at home. If Yeltsin is replaced by a new aggressive Russian nationalist, we can kiss the peace dividend good-bye." Concluding with a compliment inconsistent with his known attitude toward Bush, Nixon said, "President Bush is uniquely qualified to meet this challenge."

Nixon knew that his memo was political dynamite. To whom would it now be sent? From his famous Rolodex, he composed a list of fifty influential people and then added the spice of exclusivity by letting it be known that no one else would be getting copies. (In fact, after a few weeks, many more got copies, either directly from Nixon or faxed by friends.) Among the recipients were Henry Kissinger, Zbigniew Brzezinski, Brent Scowcroft, Safire, Hugh Sidey of *Time,* and Arnaud de Borchgrave of the *Washington Times.* (Interestingly, neither Schlesinger, who was arranging his conference, nor Baker, then Secretary of State, was on Nixon's "A" list.) The memos left New Jersey in two batches—one dated February 25, 1992, and the other dated March 3, 1992, a week later.

A personal note accompanied each copy of the memo. It began with a handwritten salutation ("Dear Zbig," "Dear Bill," "Dear Henry") and contained a terse typed message: "I have enclosed some thoughts on a vital issue that deserves priority attention during the '92 campaign." The notes were all signed, "Sincerely, RN." Nowhere on the notes or memos was there any warning label such as "Secret" or "Confidential" or "For Your Eyes Only." If Nixon had intended to limit distribution in any way, this most compulsively secretive of men could easily have stated his desire, and his "A" list probably would have complied. No, Nixon wanted the memo to leak; he just didn't want to be fingered as the one who did the leaking. Nor did he want Simes or Strmecki to leak it. He wanted to be able to disown responsibility while at the same time seeding the political atmosphere with copies of his memo so that a leak was inevitable. Simes said, "He was obviously prepared to go some distance, to take some chance, to get his views aired."

This was clearly a risky strategy. Why would Nixon want to embarrass an incumbent Republican president at a time of maximum political vulnerability? Simes said, "It would have been out of character for Nixon to do anything that would undermine the president." Yet why would Nixon offend Bush while the president was still considering whether to appear at the conference? Why anger him while there was still a chance that Nixon would be invited to the GOP National Convention in Houston? And what if the memo leaked after Bush had agreed to attend the conference, in which case the president would have been justified in believing that he had been "sandbagged" or "mousetrapped," to use Schlesinger's colorful verbs? Calculating the odds carefully, Nixon must have figured that even if the president did get "mousetrapped," he could hardly withdraw his acceptance and refuse to attend the conference without at the same time providing Nixon, Buchanan, and the Democrats with more political ammunition to use against him.

Another explanation was advanced by Leonard Garment. He felt that Nixon, far from seeking to embarrass Bush, was actually trying to help him—indeed, that the memo (and all of its intended consequences, from the leak to the impact on public policy) was part of a well-orchestrated plan conceived by Nixon and executed by Scowcroft with Bush's full knowledge and approval.

Remember, Garment advised, "Nixon's got a lot of moves. He's the Magic Johnson of politics. What else does he have to do? He sits in New Jersey—scribbling, scribbling, talking, talking. It's his last pleasure—his final pleasure. If he were in intensive care, the only part that would continue working would be his brain. He has this ability to give a sharp focus to an issue, to make a policy more acceptable to the American people." Garment seemed to enjoy his own colorful analysis. "There's an air of stagecraft about this memo. I think there was planning in this one—between Nixon and Bush. Let's face it: if this were simply a matter of Nixon bashing Bush, there'd be a lot more anger, background stories detailing the President's humiliation. No, this was public theater without Joseph Papp. Nixon is a dramatist—he's much more Machiavelli than he is Woodrow Wilson" (interview, Leonard Garment, July 1, 1992).

This argument might be persuasive but for one thing: every other person I interviewed for this project was convinced that there was no collaboration between Nixon and Bush. The president, they said, would never have allowed himself to be deliberately embarrassed and humiliated during the primaries just because Nixon wanted to accelerate an aid program for Russia. Obviously, foreign aid was less important to Bush than it was to Nixon. These two old warriors spoke the same language of Republican politics, but on this issue they did not understand each other. Bush put nothing ahead of his reelection, and Nixon put nothing ahead of his rehabilitation.

From the moment of his return to San Clemente in August 1974, Nixon had been struggling relentlessly to wash away the stain of Watergate. A contentious national debate on aid to Russia seemed at this point to be the right issue to cap this effort. It was in his ballpark, foreign affairs. It seemed virtuous. Indeed, it seemed like an all-American response to a terrible Russian crisis. Herbert Hoover, another Republican, had led a famine relief effort to the Soviet Union in the early 1920s. Nixon now wanted to lead a crusade to help the new Russia. It made news. He made news. Nixon was back!

ENTER THE PRESS

Up to this point, Nixon had been maneuvering primarily behind the scenes, plotting a strategy aimed at forcing the president to lead a major Western aid effort for Russia. Now it was the time to go public. But how? How does one take a strategy and transform it into governmental policy?

Enter the press—and all the chaos and competition, the legwork and deadlines, chance and coincidence, economic pressures and professional ethics, new and old styles, that go along with it. The press is one of America's most cherished and coddled institutions, yet at the same time one of its most criticized and distrusted. Since freedom of the press is guaranteed by the First Amendment, it is the only big business in the country explicitly protected by the U.S. Constitution. Yet academic studies and public opinion polls show that the press is in a running battle with Congress for the title of least admired actor on the national stage. If there were a vote today, the likelihood exists that the First Amendment would not be adopted and the press would not enjoy constitutional protection.

To borrow a phrase from the old sage Nathan Detroit, the press is "the oldest established permanent floating crap game" in American politics, and few politicians played the game more skillfully than Nixon. He was always prepared to denounce the press, but when it suited his purpose, he was equally prepared to exploit the press. From the Checkers speech in 1952 to the "Who lost Russia?" memo in 1992, the press had been an indispensable tool for Nixon.

In early February 1992, he again turned to *Time*. Like many professional writers, Nixon was not above recycling his material—in this case, his memo. He asked Marin Strmecki to call Richard Duncan of *Time* to see whether he would be interested in running another column on the increasingly important need for Western aid to Russia. Even though, only a few weeks before, on January 13, 1992, *Time* had run a similar column, Nixon thought the odds were good that it would accept his offer. He was right. Duncan respected Nixon's "very, very serious foreign policy mind" and, at the time, persuaded himself, after a talk with his senior editor Henry Muller, that the two columns were sufficiently different to justify publication. As Ronald Kriss, Duncan's colleague, later explained: "The issue had gathered force, and we thought the column was worth running."

Perhaps the second Nixon column, which appeared on March 9, 1992, was "worth running" because the issue of Western aid to Russia had "gathered force," but surely not because it significantly advanced the argument that Nixon had set forth in his January 13 column for *Time*. Both columns stressed the importance of large-scale Western aid to Russia, of Yeltsin's retaining power as a bulwark against the rise of a nationalistic dictator, of democracy succeeding in Russia as a way of ensuring its ultimate triumph everywhere. Neither column was critical of Bush; neither contained the sharp language, not to mention the cutting sarcasm, found in the memo. Indeed, when Duncan and Kriss read the new Nixon column, they had no idea that the memo even existed. They had not talked to Nixon; they had talked only to his aide, Strmecki, and Strmecki did not go beyond his limited brief. Therefore, the two editors did not know that at the same time they were accepting a softer version of the memo, the memo itself was being circulated to many of Nixon's associates and contacts. They were obviously not on Nixon's "A" list; neither had received a copy of the memo. Later, Kriss conceded: "Actually, we were chagrined to hear about the memo. It had quite a good kick to it." Duncan was blunter. "We were really pissed off. He scooped himself and he scooped us. I almost called him back—but didn't. The memo was much more controversial, and it obviously reflected what his game was. We were out there looking very naive, academic, while he was really putting it to Bush."

Was it possible that magazine competition had driven Duncan to run a second Nixon column? *Time*'s major competitor, *Newsweek,* had run a column on the same subject by Henry Kissinger in its February 10, 1992, issue. Duncan, when asked, said that Kissinger/*Newsweek* had nothing to do with Nixon/*Time*— indeed, that he had not even known about the Kissinger column. Still, to the reader, it seemed as if Kissinger was answering Nixon; and then Nixon, Kissinger. In his piece, the former Secretary of State criticized both the Bush and Nixon approaches to the question of aiding Russia. Kissinger accused the administration of being "hesitant," exhibiting an "ambivalence" and "a subconscious impatience with the emergence of multiple sovereignties." He charged that the United States had been "remarkably slow in dealing with the new republics" and too solicitous of Russia's wounded dignity.

While Kissinger recognized Russia as "an appropriate partner in world affairs and a major country with legitimate security interests" (words chosen with care to denote a certain diplomatic coolness and detachment), he disagreed with Nixon about opening a large-scale aid program to Russia at this time. Not until Russia demonstrated a healthy respect for the new borders of her transformed neighborhood would Kissinger consider aid, and then only in very limited amounts. Kissinger was grudging in his admiration for the new Russia; by comparison, Nixon seemed exuberant.

Time and *Newsweek* may have been competing in nonstaff experts, in who had bagged the bigger name. But it is just as likely, even more likely, that the publication of the Nixon and Kissinger columns was pure coincidence, each magazine driven by its own tastes and requirements. American journalism follows no single libretto. Though there are obvious similarities between *Time* and *Newsweek,* they still tend to march to different drummers. What is news for one may not necessarily be news for the other.

By the time the *Time* column ran on March 9, the Nixon memo had already been in the hands of a number of experienced journalists and competitors, but for a variety of different reasons, it had not yet exploded into print.

For example, de Borchgrave of the *Washington Times* got his own copy and read it, but did not write a word about it, nor did he assign one of his reporters to write about it. De Borchgrave, who normally has a sharp eye for news, missed its import.

Harry Rosenthal, an Associated Press reporter on temporary assignment to the White House, was puzzled one day in late February when he got a copy in the mail. Why would Nixon be sending him a copy? Rosenthal read it, found it interesting, and put it in a pile of suggested stories for the regular White House reporter. Maybe he felt that it was not really his story to do.

Safire, always sensitive to criticism that he was too close to Nixon, got his copy and spotted its significance, but decided not to write about it. He later remarked that he had written a Nixon piece a month or two earlier and did not want to overload the circuit. "I'm not his press agent at the *New York Times,*" he said.

At the *Washington Post,* it was a different story. An editor who was at the time unaware of the Nixon memo assigned David

Hoffman, who was then diplomatic correspondent, to do a long takeout on how campaign politics was constraining the administration's handling of foreign policy, including the question of Western aid to Russia. Hoffman did a lot of checking, in the course of which he found out about Nixon's memo and his criticism of President Bush. From his source Hoffman got a faxed copy of the memo. He could then have written a story focusing primarily on Nixon's criticism of Bush, and according to Bradley Graham, the assistant managing editor, it would "almost certainly" have been put on the front page.

But Hoffman had his editor's original, more broadly defined mandate in mind, and he stuck to it. He decided to include the Nixon criticism, but deep in the body of the story. Not until the eleventh paragraph of a long story—1,524 words, to be exact—did Hoffman even mention the memo or its criticism. He wrote, "Former President Richard M. Nixon, in a memo to friends last week that was made available to *The Washington Post,* was sharply critical of what he described as the administration's 'pathetically inadequate response' in light of the opportunities and dangers we face in the crisis in the former Soviet Union." He cited another Nixon quote but that was all. It was a decision he would later regret, but he told me that, at the time, he thought the memo "deserved a wider framework. His [Nixon's] voice was only one among many." True, but that missed the point.

Nixon was a very special critic. He was a former president, whose unique distinction was that he had resigned to avoid impeachment for his Watergate crimes. He would forever be a controversial figure. He was, in addition, a Republican, and he was attacking Bush, a fellow Republican and a protégé who was in a tough fight for reelection. Buchanan was looking for any ammunition to use against the administration. Nixon's attack was news, and Hoffman and the *Post* misplayed the story.

Hoffman finished his story on Thursday, March 5, but his editors held up publication, waiting for either a lighter news day or a better news peg. Or, maybe—who knows?—they did not read the story carefully, or they did and still missed the point. Later, Graham acknowledged that he had made a mistake. The *Post* should have insisted that Hoffman rewrite his story and lead with the Nixon criticism, "but I have to tell you that at the time it just didn't seem so urgent." Was anyone upset? "No," Graham said, "we didn't talk to David about it, and there was no recrimination. Look, there are so many stories written and edited that if we went back and looked at all of them, we'd get nothing else done." Hoffman and his editors offered the usual explanations about time, space, and news judgment, but ultimately it was Hoffman's decision and his editors agreed.

At this point the Nixon memo had been circulating in Washington and New York for about ten days, but despite its obvious news value, it had still not found its way into print. When it finally did leak, on March 10, 1992, it flooded the landscape and transformed the debate on Western aid to Russia. The *New York Times* ran two prominently placed pieces on the Nixon memo and accomplished in one edition what the former president had been orchestrating for months.

If Nixon had had the power to select the one news organization in which to feature his critique of Bush's aid policy toward Russia, he would have selected the *New York Times,* the newspaper likely to have the greatest impact. And if he had had the additional power to decide on the placement of the leak, he would have selected the front page and the op-ed page, and he ended up with both.

One *Times* story, written by Thomas Friedman, then the paper's diplomatic reporter, ran on the front page under the headline "Nixon Scoffs at Level of Support for Russian Democracy by

Bush." The other article ran on the op-ed page under the headline "How to Lose the Cold War"—the same headline that Nixon had selected for his memo. That piece was written by Daniel Schorr of National Public Radio. His Watergate reporting had infuriated Nixon, but ironically his reporting about the memo played right into Nixon's hands.

This was how it happened. On March 5, Mitchell Levitas, editor of the op-ed page of the *Times,* called Schorr and asked him to write an op-ed piece for March 12 about the results of Super Tuesday. Schorr accepted the assignment with alacrity. The two agreed to talk again on Monday, March 9.

Over the weekend, Schorr happened to be attending a conference about Russia at the Aspen Institute's Wye Plantation in Maryland. Don Oberdorfer, who was then only months away from retirement from the *Washington Post* after a long, distinguished career as a diplomatic correspondent, was also present. During a panel discussion, Oberdorfer mentioned that Nixon had written and circulated a memo highly critical of Bush's approach to the question of aid to Russia. This was news to most people at the conference. Oberdorfer had received his copy from Robert Oakley, a former State Department official who was then in residence at a Washington think tank called the U.S. Institute of Peace. Oberdorfer felt no hesitation about mentioning the memo because, for one thing, the conference was "off the record" and, for another, he knew that his colleague Hoffman had already written about it, even if the story had not yet been published.

Oberdorfer also mentioned that Nixon would be addressing a conference in Washington on March 11 and would undoubtedly be discussing his reservations about Bush's aid policy. He had learned from Simes that Nixon would be speaking at noon. The Nixon speech, Oberdorfer told the Aspen group, was a matter of "major importance," and, he added, "I intend to cover it."

It should be a matter of no great surprise that a reporter of Schorr's talent would instantly spot the newsworthiness of Oberdorfer's information. After the final panel on Saturday, Schorr invited Oberdorfer to drive back to Washington with him, and they discussed the conference, Nixon, Bush, and aid. Later that evening, in a telephone conversation, Schorr informed Oberdorfer that he was going to do a piece about Bush's policy and would appreciate a quote from the Nixon memo. Oberdorfer obliged and gave Schorr the quote about Bush's "pathetically inadequate response."

On Monday, March 9, Schorr telephoned Levitas, as planned. Schorr was still thinking primarily about the political piece that Levitas had originally assigned, and he suggested the theme of everyone campaigning to settle the question of who would govern in 1993 when no one, not even the president, was really governing in 1992. Schorr said that Bush was having problems both at home and abroad. The president seemed unable to come up with a policy on aid to Russia, for example. Almost as a throwaway line to support his case, Schorr told me, he added that "even Richard Nixon is criticizing the president."

Levitas's ears caught the unmistakable roar of a news story. What's that? he asked. What about Nixon? Levitas was relatively new to his job on the op-ed page of the *Times,* but he understood its unique power. He had been an editor of the *Times Book Review* before executive editor Max Frankel asked him in January 1991 to replace Leslie Gelb, who was about to be appointed a *Times* columnist. Levitas wanted to put his own imprint on the op-ed page, commissioning long and controversial articles from prominent people. He wanted not just their opinions but, at least as important, their insights into breaking news, such as a long Gary Sick piece on April 15, 1991, which produced flashes of public argument, suggesting a Bush connection to the 1980 negotiation allegedly holding up the release of American hostages from Iran. (Bush and others hotly denied the connection.) It was in this context that Nixon was on Levitas's list of big-name writers whose work he would like to feature on the op-ed page.

So when Schorr mentioned Nixon, Levitas was eager to hear more. Schorr explained that he had heard that Nixon had written a memo critical of the president's approach to aiding Russia and that Nixon might well go public with his criticism at a Washington conference on Wednesday. Levitas asked the obvious: could Schorr get a copy of the memo and use the Nixon criticism as the basis of his projected piece?

In fact, Schorr already had a copy. Early Monday morning, he had played a hunch, called his friend Safire and told him what he had learned about the Nixon memo. Did Safire by any chance have a copy? (Quite often, journalists get "news" from other journalists.) Yes, and within a few minutes Schorr also had a copy. Safire faxed it to his home, along with a request that if Schorr wanted to use it, fine, but first check with Nixon. Schorr was not exactly a Nixon favorite, having once earned a place of honor on his "enemies list," but what did he have to lose?

Schorr told the Nixon aide who answered the phone in his New Jersey office that he had "access" to the memo, thought it was "interesting and very well written," and wondered whether Nixon would mind if he "quoted from it." Schorr assumed that the glasnost era had not yet hit Nixon's corner of the Garden State and the aide would say that she first had to check with Nixon, and Nixon, remembering Schorr's tough broadcasts during the Watergate scandal, would probably say no; but in fact all she did say was, according to Schorr, "Sure, he'd be very happy if you did."

Delighted, Schorr informed Levitas. He knew, as he would later concede, that "I was fulfilling the master's [Nixon's] wish," but he had no journalistic qualms. Nor did Levitas. On the spot Levitas decided that Schorr should focus on the Nixon memo, but instead of publishing the piece on Thursday, March 12, as originally scheduled, it would be published the very next morning, Tuesday, March 10, the day before Nixon was to speak at his own conference. Via the op-ed page of the *New York Times,* the Nixon memo would become the herald of the Nixon speech.

Levitas, between calls, then busied himself with the morning mail. There, among the handouts and bills, was, of all things, a copy of the Nixon memo addressed to him. In recent months, Levitas had been in touch with Nixon's office about a possible op-ed piece on virtually any subject—but, though he did not get a piece, he did apparently get on Nixon's "A" or "B" list. Levitas did not have much time to relish the ironic coincidence of events. For a moment he seriously considered dropping the Schorr piece and running the Nixon memo. After all, he now had his own copy of it and it had no restrictions. He telephoned Schorr and asked, in effect, "What do I need you for?" But he decided to stick to his original plan, urging Schorr to make certain that he focused almost exclusively on the Nixon criticism of Bush's policy.

Levitas then arranged for Friedman to get his copy of the Nixon memo. It was official company policy that the op-ed page was not to scoop the front page. Levitas called Safire and asked him to run off another copy and give it to his Washington colleague down the hall. At the same time, Howell Raines, then Washington bureau chief of the *Times,* got a copy from Roger Stone, who told me that he had been instructed by Nixon to "leak" the memo to the *Times.* Raines and Stone had occasionally exchanged information in the past. This time, Stone attempted to use Raines, but by the time he delivered the memo, the *Times* was already, thanks to Schorr, Safire, and Levitas, in full gallop toward publication.

Friedman, a two-time winner of the Pulitzer Prize for his reporting from Lebanon and Israel, read the memo and "went right
for the jugular," as he would later describe his approach to the
story. "I thought it was very important, articulate, a major news
story, and I wrote it that way." Friedman relished the widespread
judgment that it was he, not Hoffman, who had spotted the story
and written it with fire and gusto.

Like most *Times* reporters covering the State Department,
Friedman had excellent sources. He had known for months that
Secretary Baker's aides were "obsessed" by a political nightmare:
that if Russia collapsed into chaos, Baker would be stuck with part
of the blame, maybe all of it. And if one day he wanted to run for
president, he would have to explain his role. It was clear to Friedman that they were relieved to learn that the *Times* intended to
focus on Nixon's criticism of Bush, not of Baker. They wanted to
protect their man, even at the risk of hurting the president. They
were also relieved to learn that Nixon had not openly criticized
Baker, although they had known for more than a year that Nixon
was angry with the Secretary of State.

During Nixon's 1991 visit to Moscow, Baker had sought to undermine his stature. He told the Russians that Nixon was a "private citizen" carrying no special messages, and he left Ambassador Jack Matlock with the impression that Matlock should not
meet Nixon at the airport. It was not a direct order, and Matlock,
encouraged by Simes, decided to greet Nixon anyway and invite
him to drive into Moscow in a U.S. Embassy limousine. In
protocol-conscious Moscow, the Matlock gesture carried the implication that Nixon had official approval. In fact he had none.
Officials at both the White House and the State Department had
told Simes that Baker wanted to dominate the aid issue and did
not appreciate Nixon's help or advice.

When Friedman sat down to write his story on Monday afternoon, he felt fully justified in leading with the Nixon-bashes-Bush
bombshell. "It was a superb story," he later told me.

Across town, in the offices of the *Washington Post*, familiar to
those who saw the movie version of *All the President's Men*, Bradley
Graham and his colleague Karen de Young, both former foreign
correspondents and now senior editors, decided to run the
Hoffman story in Tuesday's edition of the paper. Their decision
was made at just about the same time that Levitas was urging
Schorr to finish his op-ed piece for Tuesday's edition of the *Times*
and getting Friedman to do his hard-news story for Tuesday's paper as well. Both the *Post* and the *Times* were aiming for publication on March 10. The motivation of the *Post* editors was not to
beat the Nixon speech into print, which was clearly Levitas's aim,
but, rather, to give a broader foreign dimension to Super Tuesday
coverage. The headline that topped the Hoffman piece read, "U.S.
Politics Constrains Role Abroad; Voters Look Inward; World
Seeks Help."

Neither the *Times* nor the *Post* had knowledge of the other's
plans. Yet both ran their Nixon stories on the same day. Stretching
coincidence one step further, both stories ran the day before the
Nixon conference. In an age of skepticism and distrust of press
and politics, even a sophisticated reader might conclude that there
had to have been a degree of cooperation between these two great
newspapers. The fact is, there was no cooperation, no collaboration, no conspiracy. On a story of such political and diplomatic
importance as the Nixon memo, individual initiative and judgment were paramount, and coincidence and old-fashioned competition drove the game.

On Tuesday morning, March 10, President Bush saw the Friedman, Schorr, and Hoffman stories in the *Times* and the *Post*. Did
the word "conspiracy" pop into his mind? Did he denounce

Nixon more than he did the press? At a news conference at the White House, the president took the high ground and engaged in the time-honored practice of damage control. Choosing his words carefully, he said that he had talked with Nixon, that the two of them were in "total agreement," and that in any case the administration had already done a great deal to help Russia—a point flatly contradicting Nixon's basic critique.

Bush explained: "There are certain fiscal financial constraints on what we can do, but we have a huge stake in the success of democracy in Russia. . . . We will be working in every way possible to support the forces of democracy. . . . So there's a lot of taxpayer money going in this already." The president stated that he did not regard the memo as an attack on him. "I didn't take it as personally critical, and I think he would reiterate that it wasn't."

Nixon finally had the president's attention—and the press's. He had written his memo, and the memo had leaked. Then, by covering the controversy spawned by the leak, the press advanced Nixon's agenda by simply doing its job. That evening, the Nixon-Bush flap was a major story on the NBC "Nightly News." "It's Super Tuesday," began anchor Tom Brokaw, "and guess who's back? Richard Nixon. His target this time—George Bush. The consummate Cold Warrior now says an historic opportunity is being missed to help Russia." John Dancy, NBC's diplomatic correspondent, quoted extensively from the memo, major sections of which had appeared in the two *Times* stories. He himself did not have a copy. He said that Bush was "under attack," and though the president had tried to downplay his differences with Nixon, Dancy concluded that the Democrats—and Buchanan—had been given "a juicy political morsel."

The Nixon memo was a big story on the international wires, an even bigger story in Moscow. CNN, which often these days sets the standard for other news organizations, announced that it would carry the Nixon speech "live"—meaning his conference message on Russian aid the next day would encircle the globe and reach every foreign ministry in the world.

Since the Nixon memo was big news by any journalistic standard, how does one explain the fact that an estimated fifty people in New York and Washington, including many journalists, had the memo but it remained unpublished until the *Times* acted? Was it simply an example of "pack journalism" at its worst? No one wrote until everyone wrote? Was it an example of "inside the Beltway" news judgment, of no reporter or editor being able to see the forest for the trees? Was it somehow a mistaken assumption that the memo was "off the record," even though the covering note contained no such prohibition? Or was it that some journalists did not want to play any role in Nixon's political games, while a few others felt so honored to get a personal note from a former president—Nixon, no less—that they never considered its news implications?

Given the nature of American journalism, it may be that it is not possible to come up with the right answer to any of these questions. But if there was an example of a professionally correct response to the Nixon memo, it was the response in this case of the *New York Times*. As Friedman told me months later, referring to the *Post*'s Hoffman, "Remember, I got it right, and he didn't. Sometimes it's that simple."

But what does it mean to get the story "right"? Right, simply because the facts were correct? Or because the story ended up on the front page, attracting the attention of the political establishment and embarrassing the *Washington Post*, which buried its reference to Nixon's criticism? Or is there a more traditional definition: that the story was "right" because it was newsworthy, dealing with conflict between powerful people or institutions, likely to catch the reader's interest?

Friedman framed his story as a sharp difference of opinion between Nixon and Bush about aid to Russia, and *Times* editors gave it front-page play, which instantly ratified Nixon's criticism as a major story. Other news organizations naturally followed the *Times'* lead. Nixon wanted controversy—and he got it.

Media critics are often confounded by the moral neutrality of the press. If reporters know that they are being manipulated by a politician for his own ends, why do they play his game? Why do they not use their critical faculties and ask whether the game is worth the candle or whether it serves some higher purpose?

Reporters often respond to such criticism by saying that the public can worry about morality, politicians about impact, and scholars about the future of democracy; reporters need worry only about the relevance and validity of the news they present. Traditionally, they strive for objectivity. They sometimes fall short. There have been occasions, such as the coverage of "ethnic cleansing" in Bosnia, when some journalists have written their stories for the specific purpose of affecting national policy. Deborah Amos of ABC News and National Public Radio, speaking at the Kennedy School on April 7, 1994, acknowledged that while covering Bosnia she and a number of her colleagues had written the story with a view toward changing U.S. and NATO policy from diplomatic pressure to military action against Serbian forces.

To the degree that this change in professional attitude is simply a limited response to the anguish of covering a truly dreadful human tragedy such as the events in Bosnia, this may be understandable, though still regrettable. But if reporters are now to adopt a moral attitude toward their stories, then the public is almost certain to be shortchanged. Nixon may be a despised figure to those Americans who remember the Watergate scandal and place him beyond the pale of respectable coverage, but he made news when he wrote his memo attacking the Bush administration, and deserved the coverage. Detachment from the news for reasons of moral revulsion is not a luxury the press can afford.

Levitas recognized that Nixon was a master of press manipulation and that, by running the memo, the op-ed page of the *Times* was serving his ends, even lending its enormous prestige and credibility to his message, but that in the final analysis if Nixon was making news—and in this case he surely was—the *Times* had an obligation to cover the news and run it. That's the job of journalism. Nixon understood that job better than many other politicians, and he had no hesitation about using the press to advance his own agenda.

Indeed, the mark of a modern-day, television-and-news-oriented politician is recognition of the strengths and weaknesses of journalism. The skilled politician recognizes a journalist's professional need for news and provides it. The politician knows in advance that even if the information is recognized as self-serving, the journalist is almost certain to use it anyway. The journalist cannot escape the professional obligation to pursue and use news, even if it is being served up on a silver platter, even if the quality of political exploitation is as obvious as a summer storm. News is news.

Nixon intuitively understood the vibrations of American journalism: what it needs, what it can use. Nixon surveyed the political horizon in early March 1992 and, as Stone later put it, "sprung the trap." His memo was now network and front-page news. Tomorrow the conference, another major piece of the Nixon strategy, would begin, and at the conference Nixon would see to it that the press would again play a pivotal role.

7

THE CONFERENCE: FIRST, NIXON . . .

On March 11–12, 1992, the main ballroom of the Four Seasons Hotel in Washington, D.C., was the setting for "America's Role in the Emerging World," a "National Policy Conference" sponsored by the "Richard Nixon Library and Birthplace." The star was clearly Nixon. Not since his resignation in August 1974 had there been a Washington conference in his honor. Not since then had the American people been so ready, judging by the polls, to restore the former president to a position of public esteem.

Dimitri Simes and James Schlesinger worked on the final details. Several hundred senior officials, former and present, diplomats, scholars, and journalists—Nixon's extended family, in a sense—had been invited. Guest lists had been checked and rechecked. Protocol was extremely important. Propinquity to Nixon became a measuring rod of power. Who would sit at the head table? Who would sit at the tables closest to Nixon's?

Press coverage was no longer a concern. By publishing the memo on March 10, the *Times* had served the role of a highly respectable Washington tip sheet. Other newspapers, wire services, radio, and television followed its lead and featured piggyback stories about Nixon's criticism of Bush's policy on aid to Russia. The conference was now certain to attract widespread attention, both in the United States and abroad.

As far as Nixon was concerned, Bush's presence was crucially important. He wanted a presidential seal of approval, even if it was to be given by a politician whom he still regarded as a "candy ass" elitist. Simes and Schlesinger were keenly aware of Nixon's desire to get the president of the United States to attend this conference. They had been in frequent contact with the White House, pleading for a positive response. At one time, they had gotten what sounded like a rejection, but they kept lobbying with friends at the White House, the Pentagon, and Congress for Bush to attend.

Bush had his own priorities, different from Nixon's. The period after the New Hampshire primary on February 18 was a time of despair and disarray at the White House. The president found it hard to focus on his campaign. He still had not gotten over the shock of the special Senate election in Pennsylvania a few months earlier, when a relatively unknown Democrat, Harris Wofford, had beaten his attorney general, Dick Thornburgh, causing the president to panic and postpone a scheduled trip to Asia. Throughout the South, Buchanan kept pounding away at Bush, attracting not only large and enthusiastic crowds but also time on the evening TV news programs. He did not win a single primary, but he did win 20–25 percent of the Republican vote and warned that the word "quit" did not exist in his vocabulary. Bush did not want to seem to be interested in foreign affairs, his long suit, when Democrat Clinton and Buchanan were focusing on domestic affairs and when the polls showed a popular preoccupation with the economy.

Still, in the end, Bush decided that he did not want to offend Nixon, who represented conservative power in the Republican Party. On March 2, Bush called Nixon's daughter, Julie Eisenhower, and, according to Simes, told her that he would be "delighted" to speak at the conference on the evening of March 11. At almost the same time, calls went from Scowcroft's office to

Simes and Schlesinger confirming the president's acceptance. A feeling of vindication swept over Nixon. There he was, finally, back in the big leagues.

Leonard Garment put Nixon's "return" in biblical terms: "He has passed through the valley of the shadow of Watergate." He then added: "For some people, Nixonphobia is a kind of fixation. But most of the country has absorbed Watergate and made it a part of history." Charles Krauthammer, the Washington columnist whom Nixon had thanked for inspiring the "Who lost Russia?" threat, observed: "The statute of limitations on Watergate has run out."

Like many other conferences in Washington, this one covered weighty topics, such as "U.S. Global Involvement: Is It Worth the Price?" and "The United States and the End of the Soviet Union." For panelists and speakers, it drew prominent personalities, such as Zbigniew Brzezinski, Senator Warren Rudman, and Henry Kissinger—the sort of stars who appeared not just on C-Span but on the larger commercial networks, too. What added an extra dose of news luster to this conference was Nixon's dramatic comeback as a controversial critic of an incumbent president's policy toward the new Russia.

Shortly before noon, after the first panel had concluded its work, a bank of television lights suddenly snapped to life, alerting everyone to the imminence of Nixon's arrival. It was as if he were still president. He entered from the rear, that familiar smile on his face—to quote reporter David Remnick, "that great landscape of jowl, slope and plane." He shook hands with admiring guests as he made his way to a front table. He walked slowly, one foot dragging slightly. Everyone was standing, applauding. Former aides were thrilled, former "enemies" thought it was time to turn over a new leaf, few felt indifferent. It was clear to everyone that this was to be a memorable Washington event. Daughter Julie was jubilant.

"We couldn't be sure this day would come. But I never stopped believing."

After a lunch of grilled salmon, Schlesinger rose and introduced the main speaker. "Mr. Nixon's place in history," he said, "will be undergirded by his acknowledged skills in foreign policy. Today, many foreign leaders feel it worthwhile to make a pilgrimage to benefit from his enormous experience." Then Schlesinger made the only oblique reference to Watergate that one heard at the conference. "Our speaker is a man who has weathered a storm that would have been fatal to most other men. . . . Mr. President, tell us about the world."

Nixon then spoke for thirty-five minutes to a hushed house. He stood on a platform flanked by two plump green plants so perfectly manicured they looked fake. His only prop was a standing microphone—no lectern, no notes. His theme was by now familiar to anyone who had read *Time,* the *New York Times,* or the memo. Foreign policy was extraordinarily important, but there had been no discussion of it during the presidential campaign, not even of the historic revolution sweeping through Russia. Nixon made the rather obvious point that foreign and domestic policy were one. He reached into history for a parallel that he hoped reporters would note. Winston Churchill's famous "Iron Curtain" speech, he said, had been delivered "exactly 45 years ago today." Nixon was off by a year and six days, but who cared? Churchill had addressed the challenge of the old Russia. Nixon would now address the challenge of the new Russia.

For openers, Nixon again stressed the crucial importance of Boris Yeltsin's ascent to the Russian presidency. Even though foreign aid was not popular in the United States, especially during a recession, he thought the West should organize an urgent aid program to help Yeltsin transform a stultified economy into a free market and in the process boost the chances of democracy. "All of the pollsters are telling their candidates," Nixon said, "'Don't tackle foreign policy, and particularly foreign aid, because foreign aid is poison as a political issue.' They're wrong and history proves it."

About America's role in this crusade, Nixon asked a series of rhetorical questions. "If America does not lead, who? The Japanese? Chinese? Russians? Germans? This is our moment of greatness. It's our moment of truth. We must seize this moment because we hold the future in our hands."

If the United States failed to "lead," then Russia would almost surely reach into its reactionary past and produce a new tsar or Stalin. "That new despotism," Nixon warned, "would be a far more dangerous threat to peace and freedom in the world . . . than was the old Soviet totalitarianism." Once again, Nixon set up a misleading dichotomy between Yeltsin and democracy on one hand and "a new despotism" on the other, as though they represented the only alternatives in Russia's uncertain future.

How much would the Nixon program cost? That was the question on many minds. At his press conference the day before, President Bush had placed particular emphasis on America's limited financial reach to explain his administration's limited response to Russia's needs. Nixon did not offer his own figure, instead citing the *New York Times*' and the *Financial Times*' estimates that it would cost $20 billion a year over a three- to five-year period. He argued that, by comparison, the West had spent twenty times that amount in 1990 alone simply to defend itself against Russia. In other words, the aid program would be a very solid investment. Cheap, by comparison. Then he referred to one of his favorite stories and cited the path-breaking courage of a Democratic president in forging the Truman Doctrine to protect Greece and Turkey after World War II. He suggested that similar political courage was needed now.

"I remember as if it were yesterday Harry Truman jaunting [*sic*], some said a little cocky, coming down before a joint session of Congress and asking for millions of dollars in aid to Greece and Turkey to prevent Communist subversion and possibly Communist aggression." Nixon then embraced the example of another Democrat to strengthen his argument. "It was a very tough vote for two very young, and both, as history later indicated, rather ambitious young Congressmen. The liberal Democrats in Jack Kennedy's Massachusetts district were against any military foreign aid. And the conservative Republicans in my California district were against all foreign aid. Under the circumstances, however, after considering it, we both voted for it."

Perhaps without even being aware of it, Nixon started an extraordinary political and journalistic craze in the 1992 campaign: the adoption of Harry Truman—a man he had bitterly opposed—by the Republican Party and its presidential candidate. Though Bush had voted against Truman in 1948 and opposed his philosophical approach to government and civil rights, he cynically wrapped both arms around the Truman legacy of the underdog battling Congress and winning reelection. On Labor Day, 1992, Bush invoked the name of Truman—not Reagan, Nixon, or Eisenhower—to launch his general election campaign. On the same day, more appropriately, Governor Bill Clinton of Arkansas went to Independence, Missouri, Truman's hometown, to kick off his successful campaign for the presidency.

Not once during his talk did Nixon directly criticize Bush, nor did he repeat the withering criticism of administration policy toward Russia that had been in his memo. It was unnecessary. The *New York Times* had already trumpeted his message. NBC News and many other news organizations had joined in the chorus. Nixon had targeted Bush, and Bush was suddenly trapped in the bright lights of a Nixon "double hit," as Simes had put it—first the memo and now the conference. Could the president still resist the pressure to launch an aid program for Russia?

It was a virtuoso performance. The standing ovation, the press play, and Bush's reaction were testimony to Nixon's ability still to affect an important matter of public policy. But there remained questions about the substance of his presentation.

Was Nixon propounding some radically new doctrine of international relations? Not really. Foreign aid, even on a massive scale, had been tested with uneven results since the beginning of the Cold War. Yes, but what about aid to Russia? Even this was not new. American aid flowed to Russia after the Bolshevik Revolution and during World War II. Moreover, an aid program to the new, post-Communist Russia had already been discussed in many settings: at the G-7 meetings, in Congress, in university seminars, even at the White House; and Congress had already appropriated limited funds for economic and humanitarian aid to the former Soviet Union.

Nixon, a politician whose global views were formed by his experiences in World War II and the Cold War, seemed to consider aid to Russia in much the same category as Marshall Plan aid to Western Europe in the late 1940s. The pre-war economies of France, Germany, Italy, and their neighbors were essentially based on market principles, and they could absorb foreign aid to rebuild their devastated countries. Aid to Russia was a totally different proposition. The fundamental problem there, after the collapse of Communism, was to construct a market economy on the ruins of a command system. Only then could large-scale foreign aid have a chance of making a positive, meaningful impact on the economy.

This difference between the Marshall Plan and the Nixon Plan was ignored by the former president. His speeches, articles, and books strongly suggest that up to that point he had not given serious consideration to the complexity or applicability of a massive aid program for Russia. One critic later said: "Aid to Russia is not like aid to Biafra; it's not just a matter of paying for flour and antibiotics. . . . Piping dollars into the present system is hardly going to put pressure on the system to change."

There were other questions, too, rarely asked in the wide-eyed admiration of the moment. Was Nixon providing any new insights into Russian politics? Again, not really. An authoritarian ruler could certainly replace Yeltsin. Indeed, given Russia's history, pre- and postrevolutionary, such a scenario would be likely. But it was far from the only likelihood in the midst of Russia's current upheaval. Was the question of "Who lost Russia?" helpful? Was it, for that matter, even accurate as a way of forecasting the tone and quality of American politics in the 1990s? Was it an especially penetrating question? Or was it designed simply to frighten the president and those in Congress who had a different vision of American priorities? Even so, was it an effective tool for ginning up support for Russia?

By any objective standard, Nixon's speech, while important for its time, did not deserve the enthusiastic response that it generated. Normally cautious analysts embraced his argument before they bothered to examine its substance. The speech was neither brilliant nor original. It was not marked by the sort of historical or philosophical insights found in the speeches of a Churchill or a de Gaulle, those statesmen with whom Nixon always linked himself. Nixon seemed striking and unusual primarily because of the sharp contrast between his political style and that of Reagan and Bush, between the drama and excitement of the 1960s and 1970s and the disappointment and retrenchment of the 1980s and 1990s.

Nixon spoke without notes or teleprompter for thirty-five minutes. Reagan, by contrast, always found the chalk mark and never uttered an unscripted thought. Often, within minutes after the conclusion of one of his news conferences, his spokespersons would come cruising through the newsroom issuing "clarifications" designed to correct the president, and no one seemed embarrassed. Teflon protected him but ultimately damaged the Oval Office. The teleprompter on two reflecting pieces of glass, one on either side of the speaker's podium, has become an omnipresent symbol of the modern presidency. Throughout the 1992 campaign, Bush seemed always to be hunched over a portable podium, peering at the teleprompter or clutching five-by-seven cards as if his message, no less than his political life, depended upon them.

Andrew Glass, Washington bureau chief for Cox Newspapers, explained that the coin of the political realm had been generally debased over the years, as power shifted to new centers. Speechwriters, handlers, experts, manipulators—they controlled a president as if he were on remote control. So, Glass said, "when politicians appear genuine, when suddenly things seem to be not an artifice, one is then impressed, perhaps inordinately." In this context, Nixon seemed to be, as Garment said, "the last of the old-timers," a throwback to the days when politicians, according to Schlesinger, "just spoke."

But, in fact, Nixon never "just spoke." Schlesinger recalled that many of his speeches were also "pre-scripted" and "memorized." Kissinger said that his old boss used to draft his speeches on a yellow, lined pad, commit them to memory, and then practice them before a mirror. William Hyland, once an adviser on Nixon's NSC staff, later the editor of *Foreign Affairs,* listened to the speech at the Four Seasons Hotel and immediately thought, "He's memorized it, I'm certain. It's what he always does." The difference between Nixon and his successors was that Nixon cleverly disguised his preparations.

I remembered a personal experience that confirmed this judgment. During the Nixon administration, I covered a summit in Bermuda between the president and a British prime minister. As a member of a press pool, I was with the president and the prime minister as they left the governor general's mansion on a brilliantly clear afternoon and walked toward a bullpen of reporters and cameras halfway down a rolling green lawn. Abruptly, out of camera range, Nixon stopped, while the others continued for another few steps before they, too, stopped and waited with small talk and awkward shuffles for the president to complete what seemed like a strange meditation. He stood still, his head lowered as if in deep thought. Then, as I (and I assume the others) watched in amazement, he began to mouth a string of words and to gesture vigorously, coordinating gestures with words as though he were actually making a number of important points before a live audience. This odd pantomime continued for another minute or so until, apparently satisfied, he smiled to himself, caught up with the embarrassed prime minister, walked to a podium in front of the press bullpen, and began to say out loud, with the appropriate gestures, what he had obviously just practiced. He seemed very articulate and knowledgeable. The prime minister may have been impressed, or puzzled. Who knows? Surely the reporters who hadn't seen the Nixon practice session were impressed.

Oberdorfer, who was at the conference, noted in his journal that evening: "As so often before, he had written and memorized his speech, and delivered it with the classic debater's style—gestures and all—without notes, teleprompters or a lectern—'the man in the arena' before a single mike. He must have spent a great deal of time preparing it well. He flubbed a bit, but I thought it was a good speech and very well-delivered—and to tell the truth, I enjoyed it, wallowing a bit in, what for me, was a nostalgic occasion."

Oberdorfer later greeted Nixon, whom he had covered, and Nixon asked what he was doing. "Still covering foreign affairs for the *Washington Post,*" Oberdorfer responded, according to his journal, "whereupon, he put his two hands on my shoulders, looked me in the eye and said there were many important things being said here, more important as a story than he was. 'I think this story will be about you, Mr. Nixon,' I responded with mock seriousness. And so it was."

This game of press/politics, as played at the Four Seasons Hotel, had echoes throughout Washington, the United States, and the world. Nixon and the conference sparked press interest in the question of Russian aid, the press's new interest led to more coverage, and the increased coverage influenced politicians in the White House and Congress to address the question in a more serious and urgent manner.

In Washington, on the same day as the Nixon conference, Deputy Secretary of State Lawrence Eagleburger appeared before the House Appropriations Subcommittee to explain and defend the administration's approach to helping Central and Eastern Europe. At the same time, Robert Strauss, U.S. ambassador to Moscow, appeared before the Senate Foreign Relations Committee to express his "amazement" that the Russian revolution was not being feverishly debated on Capitol Hill. And in the Senate Radio and TV Gallery, two Democratic and two Republican senators, just back from a lightning swing through Russia and Ukraine, expounded on their views about aiding the former Soviet Union.

Eagleburger in his testimony seemed to be directly answering Nixon when he stressed that the United States did not have "limitless resources." He recognized that the Russian challenge was "unprecedented," but he argued: "Simply throwing money at the situation—especially money that in these times we can ill afford to waste—will not solve these problems. Indeed, money indis-

criminately pumped into the region could hinder reform and pro-
mote the very dependencies that have for too long existed in these
countries. We must remain prudent." Eagleburger then outlined
the administration's proposals: $400 million in fiscal year 1992 and
$450 million in fiscal year 1993 for Central and Eastern Europe;
and $620 million in fiscal year 1992 and fiscal year 1993 for the
former Soviet Union, combined with $860 million from existing
legislation. Nixon had been talking about tens of billions.

That afternoon, Edward Hewett of the NSC staff disclosed at
the conference that $44 billion in Western aid had gone to the
former Soviet Union in 1990 and 1991, "and no one is sure where
it went." His point was clear: that the massive aid Nixon sought—
even if the money existed in sufficient quantity—might simply
vanish into the pit of Russian corruption and inefficiency.

At the Senate Foreign Relations Committee hearing, one senator after another referred to the Nixon memo, as it had been reported by the *Times* and other news organizations. Chairman
Claiborne Pell of Rhode Island inserted the Friedman article from
the *Times* into the *Congressional Record.* Even conservative Jesse
Helms of North Carolina supported Nixon's proposal to send
large-scale aid to what was once the heartland of the Evil Empire.
It was as if there was no longer any need to debate the merits of
the Nixon proposal. The former president encouraged liberals
and conservatives alike to help Russia. If there was an underlying
concern, it was that the administration was not demonstrating
"leadership" on the issue. Strauss, as ambassador, could not be
critical of the president, so he widened his focus and in effect
denounced everyone.

"I find it amazing to come back in the middle of a presidential
campaign," he said, "to find that a subject as important as . . . the
former Soviet Union . . . hasn't been the subject of . . . any appre-
ciable discussion at all. . . . It's just shocking to think that you're

so wrapped up, [you] think the whole world is revolving around what you're doing."

Where was the leadership? Strauss seemed to be pleading with the White House to fill the void. Choosing his examples carefully, he said, in his colorful fashion: "I've had letters from Senator Helms and Senator Thurmond, for example, two men who represent the more conservative wing of your party. Senator Helms said: 'You lead, and I'll follow. Tell me what we need to do, Bob.' And he's writing a Democratic man on that. I've had letters from the liberal Senators who sit as members of this committee and otherwise saying—I've had calls from them: 'We will—just tell us—we're ready to follow if someone leads.'"

Strauss also said: "This isn't beanbag we're playing. These are big-time issues, this is life or death, this is the future of nations."

In the Senate Radio and TV Gallery, the four senators just back from the former Soviet Union—Democrats Sam Nunn of Georgia and Jeff Bingaman of New Mexico and Republicans John Warner of Virginia and Richard Lugar of Indiana—said that they wanted to "focus and energize this Administration," to quote Nunn, to help Russia during this "unique time in history." Strongly suggesting that he had read the Nixon memo and valued the political power of "Who lost Russia?" Nunn directed his fire at Bush. "It is my view," he said, "that the place in history of President Bush will be judged by what happens in our own government in treating this as a priority over the next several months." Warner also looked toward the Oval Office. "If we were to sit on the sidelines and not seize this initiative," he said, echoing the Nixon message, "this march for democracy might be stopped and strong factions seize the governments in several of the republics. . . . We ought to exercise strong leadership."

On that day in Washington, Nixon had achieved his goal of inaugurating a major debate on the question of helping Russia.

On Capitol Hill, testimony focused on the pros and cons (mostly pros) of this issue. Reporters interviewed experts and wrote stories. CNN carried the Nixon message from one end of the world to the other. There were questions about the degree to which all of the testimony had been coincidental or carefully orchestrated to amplify or muffle the Nixon message. My own belief, after checking, was that the timing of the various presentations was coincidental but that the various participants exploited the aroused interest in Russian aid to advance their own agendas. Eagleburger, for example, tried to justify the administration's cautious response. Strauss, no slouch at political gamesmanship, took advantage of the Nixon hullabaloo to press his personal crusade for Western aid. The four senators did what came naturally to inhabitants of Capitol Hill: they cashed in on the new press interest in the Russian aid question to pressure the president to adopt their strategy.

Meanwhile, at the Four Seasons Hotel, Nixon was basking in his newfound acclaim. Others could consider such questions as coincidence or master manipulation; he was enjoying the role of statesman above politics. After his luncheon speech, reporters surrounded the former president. Why was he attacking Bush? they wanted to know. Nixon shook his head, as if the thought had never entered his mind. He was not attacking Bush, he said; he was only trying to "focus attention on what I consider to be the major foreign policy issue of our time." He added that he looked forward to what the president would have to say in his address that evening. After what had just happened in Washington, it was not only Nixon who looked forward to the Bush speech. It was also every reporter, politician, and diplomat in the city.

THE CONFERENCE: . . . AND THEN BUSH

Nixon had been a great success, and not only by his own yard-stick. His speech had attracted widespread attention. Russian Ambassador Lukin lavished praise on the former president. "Russia needs help," he said, echoing the Nixon/Yeltsin line. "The choice is Russian democracy or Russian authoritarianism." Reporters raced in and out of the Four Seasons Hotel to file their stories. Editors and producers prepared pieces for the evening news and the morning papers. CNN, with its worldwide reach, recapped the Nixon speech every hour. There seemed to be no escape from the news that Nixon was again at the center of a major Washington story. Even skeptics acknowledged that, by whatever maneuvers, Nixon had introduced the subject of aid to Russia into the presidential campaign as a matter of national interest and security. He had raised it above the level of everyday politics.

In the conference room, throughout the afternoon, many former officials from the Nixon administration circulated in pools of warm nostalgia, as they boasted about Nixon and his speech. If a vote had been taken, it would surely have been unanimous that Nixon was the most brilliant foreign policy thinker of our time. As they reminisced, they seemed to be rediscovering their own self-respect.

Safire recalled the "February Group," an occasional gathering of old Nixonians who would meet "furtively" to discuss the good old days. At the Four Seasons, Safire saw many familiar faces suddenly glowing with pride. "You can see it in the faces of the people who used to skulk around in the February Group," said Safire, not one of those who ever seemed to skulk. "His comeback is everybody else's comeback too." Lobbyist Max Friedersdorf beamed. "I haven't seen so many [Nixonians] since we left the White House." Maurice Stans, Nixon's Secretary of Commerce and finance chairman of CREEP, the Committee to Re-Elect the President, added: "No doubt about it—he's the elder statesman. Look at the other retired presidents, and see which of them plays as much of a public role as Nixon does."

While Nixon's "faithful flock," to use *Times* columnist Gelb's phrase, continued their joyful bonding at the hotel, not too far away, at 1600 Pennsylvania Avenue, Bush's advisers were in a frantic rush behind the scenes to complete the speech he was to deliver that night at the conference. The president himself was romancing reporters in the overcrowded press room. It was the day after Super Tuesday—a "great day," he said. He had swept fifteen states and wanted desperately, with these primary victories, to drive a stake through Buchanan's isolationist heart. The president said, "Americans must not heed the lone trumpets of retreat." He spoke optimistically about the economy, space exploration, and the end of the Cold War. But if he expected the White House press corps to be so bedazzled by his upbeat appraisal that they would ignore the obvious—Nixon's challenge—he was to be quickly disabused of the notion.

A reporter at the press conference asked about Nixon's "fairly scathing memo." The president reached into a pot of political latex for words that stretched the truth. Nothing new at White House briefings. "I read the Nixon paper," he responded, "and I didn't consider it scathing. . . . I think we're in very close agreement." Then he carefully defined the "one area where we

might have a difference." He said: "We're living in a time of constrained resources. There isn't a lot of money around. We're
spending too much as it already is. So to do the things I would
really like to do, I don't have a blank check for all of that." The
difference between them, Bush seemed to be saying, was only one
of degree—he, too, favored aid to Russia; it was just a matter of
how much. Many reporters felt that the president's answer to
Nixon lacked conviction.

Despite Bush's best efforts to stress the upbeat results of Super
Tuesday as one way of muffling his differences with Nixon, he
could not dispel the widespread impression that these were tough
days at the White House. Reporters sensed in the president's campaign a lack of direction, a widening disorganization, and a loss of
energy and purpose. Decisions that were once considered routine
seemed to mushroom into monumental problems, delays, stalls.
The president's own indecisiveness trickled down through the entire bureaucracy. Even with regard to the Nixon memo, it was
clear that the administration could not decide on its own message
and could not control the coverage—two signs of serious trouble
in any political operation.

Ever since March 2, 1992, when the president finally agreed to
attend the Nixon conference, no one at the White House could
decide on what kind of speech the president should deliver: one
that gushed with happy talk about Nixon (it was, after all, his day
and his conference); one that candidly disagreed with Nixon; or
one that leapfrogged his message into a new and generous administration policy toward the new Russian revolution. These were
not trivial questions. They required study and decisions, but days
passed without action and now there was no more time for
procrastination.

Nor was the Nixon memo the only major leak that week to
command White House attention. The Pentagon had just pre-

pared a forty-six-page secret study spelling out a new post–Cold War strategy for the United States, and it, too, had leaked. Defense Secretary Dick Cheney and his senior aides had concluded, according to the *New York Times* on March 8, 1992, that the United States, as the world's surviving superpower, was now intent on ensuring that no rival power would be allowed to emerge in Western Europe, Asia, or the territory of the former Soviet Union. Was the *Times* story accurate? How much would such a policy cost? How would it be implemented? Had there been any consultation with allies? With Congress? The White House ducked a direct answer.

Not for the first time, when the White House faced a difficult choice in the absence of a presidential decision, it went in two opposite directions and hoped for the best. Two drafts of a presidential speech for the Nixon conference were commissioned: one from the speechwriters, led by David Demerest; the other from the National Security Council, led by Brent Scowcroft, who turned for help to Richard Haass, one of his aides responsible for Middle East policy but also knowledgeable about Russia. Haass, who had a doctorate from Oxford and had taught at Harvard's Kennedy School of Government, had drafted other presidential statements and speeches on foreign policy. Between Demerest and Haass there were the differences and tensions that often beset the White House before a major speech.

On March 9, 1992, two days before the conference and one day before the Nixon memo exploded on the front page of the *Times,* the first drafts of the Bush speech were submitted to Scowcroft. According to one aide, Demerest's was a "bouquet" to Nixon, flowery and effusive but lacking any bite or direction on Russian policy; Haass's blasted the neo-isolationism then being trumpeted by Buchanan, without mentioning his name, and called for major U.S. support of Russian reform within the realistic constraints imposed by the American recession and the presidential campaign. Scowcroft studied both drafts. He believed that good policy made good politics. If Bush was to speak before the conference, he had better be substantive and serious. He presented the drafts to Bush. The question was simple: did the president want a Nixon speech or a foreign policy speech? Bush could not make up his mind. He wanted a foreign policy speech, he said, but one laced with admiration for Nixon.

Scowcroft interpreted the president's vagueness in his own way. He decided that the Haass draft would become the basic text, but he also told Demerest to include warm words about Nixon's significant contributions to American foreign policy. Watergate never entered anyone's mind. Over the next forty-eight hours, a single draft emerged after numerous battles between Haass and Demerest. The final draft reflected both approaches. It was highly complimentary of Nixon, while underscoring Bush's stewardship of the post–Cold War transition.

What became clear during these drafting sessions was that quite a few officials at the White House were churning with re-sentment toward Nixon and disappointment about Bush. They felt that the president had been quite generous to Nixon but that Nixon had been uncommonly selfish. It was "obvious to all of us," said one NSC official, who did not wish to be identified by name, that "Nixon's commitment to his own political recovery was paramount to him. Everyone else was dispensable, including the President." Nixon was seen as insensitive. "Didn't Nixon un-derstand the President's problems?" asked another official who likewise did not want to be named. "First the leaking of the memo, and now this conference." Eagleburger, reflecting the opinion of both Baker and other senior State Department offi-cials, spoke of Nixon's "grand-standing," and another State De-partment official exclaimed: "Nixon hijacked Washington for 48 hours and held the President hostage. He also hijacked the press, and the press allowed itself to be hijacked."

On Wednesday afternoon, Haass, with Scowcroft's approval, violated White House protocol. He began to brief reporters about the president's speech before Bush himself had cleared the final draft. Haass spoke "on background," meaning "White House officials" could be quoted but not Haass himself. Though he knew better, Haass could not resist the temptation to describe his labors as a "major speech"—the first in a long time that focused on foreign policy. He had in fact tried unsuccessfully for months to generate enthusiasm for a major speech on foreign policy: now that the Cold War was over, what should U.S. policy be? What should be its responsibilities in a new world order? Knowing every comma in the speech, Haass was under no illusion that the Bush speech, in its roughly final form, would or could steal the spotlight from Nixon. The reason was clear. The speech failed to project vision or move policy. It was a mishmash of fawning praise and inadequate policy. It was a missed opportunity. Rather than confront Nixon or project a bold new direction in foreign policy, Bush approved a draft that offended no wing of the Republican Party. It lacked fire. It inspired no one. And it did not end up making "news." According to the modern rules of press/politics, if it did not get on TV, the front page of the *New York Times,* or the news wires, it did not exist. "After all that work," Haass told a friend, "the speech had limited impact."

Why? In part because, for whatever combination of reasons, the preoccupied president did not sign off on the speech until shortly before he left the White House for the Four Seasons Hotel. The speech, when it was finally distributed to the press, had a 7:30 P.M. embargo on it—an hour after the normal embargo time. That meant that the press could not report the president's remarks until after the evening news was on television and the early editions of many major newspapers on the East Coast had gone to bed. It also meant that, since the reporters had heard the Nixon speech (or seen it on CNN or read about it on the wires) but still had no idea what the president would be saying in response, Nixon—and his message—would end up dominating the news coverage. The White House had lost not only a "news cycle" but also a golden opportunity to trump Nixon.

In this time of modern technology, with its emphasis upon the nonstop transmission of information by way of satellites, computers, fiber optic cables, cellular telephones, and fax machines, the concept of a "news cycle" has lost some of its relevance and power, but not all of it. It is still centrally important for the U.S. government, especially for a White House in pursuit of reelection. Every president wants his story-of-the-day to be on the evening news. Even though "ABC World News Tonight with Peter Jennings," the "CBS Evening News with Dan Rather," and the "NBC Nightly News with Tom Brokaw" now command only about 55–60 percent of the television audience, as compared with 75–80 percent twenty years ago, they still collectively draw the largest television audience in the early evening. Likewise, the front pages of the *Times* and the *Post* are considered crucially important. No president can be indifferent to the power of the press to help or hurt his crusade. Bush was not indifferent; he was simply outfoxed.

On the evening of March 11, 1992, the four major television networks, including CNN, had plenty of time to review and cut a relatively lengthy story about Nixon, generally within the context of a former president, a Republican, putting additional pressure on the incumbent President, also a Republican, to change a key element of his foreign policy during a tough primary campaign. Although Nixon focused on aid to Russia, the context of the TV stories was political. After all, since it was only the day after Super

Tuesday, for everyone, press and politician, the campaign was still paramount. For the second evening in a row, "NBC Nightly News" ran a Nixon piece of 1 minute 50 seconds in length. ABC ran a slightly longer piece—2 minutes 3 seconds. CBS ran its piece at 2 minutes 1 second, and CNN "PrimeNews" ran the longest piece—2 minutes 54 seconds.

In addition, the Nixon story made TV and newspaper headlines all around the world—in Canada, Britain, France, Germany, Russia, China, Japan, the Middle East, South America, Africa. A Nexis computer search revealed that the coverage was almost uniformly favorable. Nixon was treated respectfully, like the elder statesman and oracle he wanted to be. For example, the *Independent* in London said in a lead editorial on March 13, 1992, "The former Republican President, Richard Nixon, has done his country a service." An editorial in the *Los Angeles Times,* which ran on the same day, struck almost the same theme using almost the same words: "Former President Richard M. Nixon has performed a service to his country." Essayist Mark Feeney, writing in the *Boston Globe,* usually a source of blistering criticism of Nixon, now referred to him as "the most electric figure in 20th century American politics." Feeney compared Nixon to a progression of Shakespearean characters: Iago, Malvolio, Richard III, and now Prospero. From *The Tempest,* Feeney quoted, with delight, "Nothing of him that doth fade, / But doth suffer a sea-change, / Into something rich and strange."

There were a few journalists who resisted the rush to poetry, but they were such a scattered lot that they created barely a ripple of dissent. In Canada, columnist John Hay, writing in the *Ottawa Citizen,* asked, "Why flatter the loathsome Nixon?" He could not think of a single good reason, not even Nixon's emphasis on helping Russia. "The timidity of U.S. aid to Russia is so obvious that Nixon's observation is not so much acute as banal." *Times* columnist Gelb described Nixon as the "old trickster," a "phony" who seemed more interested in Russia than he did in America. The question was not, Gelb wrote on March 13, 1992, who lost Russia; "the question I would put to Nixon and his faithful flock is this: 'who is losing America?'" Gelb, like many others, believed that the administration should focus on the urgent needs of America, not Russia, and do so before it was too late.

By 7:00 P.M., most of the black-tie dinner guests had arrived for the president's speech. There was a sense of anticipation in the room. The release of the speech had been delayed; no one was certain why. Journalists began to speculate: perhaps the president, inspired by Nixon's call to greatness, had decided at the last minute that, rather than fight off the challenge of Buchanan and a weak economy with a series of defensive moves, he would boldly proclaim a new Marshall Plan—a wide-ranging program of aid to Eastern Europe and Russia that would parallel the American effort in Western Europe after World War II.

At exactly 7:15 P.M., a White House phalanx of Secret Service agents and aides swept into the room, and in its wake walked the president and Mrs. Bush. They were greeted by Nixon, Schlesinger, Tricia Nixon Cox, and Julie Nixon Eisenhower. There was some awkwardness, Nixon never certain where to keep his hands and Bush slapping convenient backs and pointing to people beyond the immediate circle, as if in recognition. Both presidents smiled broadly but with the recognizable theatricality reserved for large gatherings. Dinner consisted of filet of sole with salmon mousseline, chocolate torte, and Irish crème anglaise, and the table talk seemed animated, especially between Nixon and Mrs. Bush.

At the appropriate time, the room suddenly blazed with television lights and Nixon rose to introduce the president. The moment had come. No doubt there were those in the room who expected a diplomatic breakthrough; others, more realistic, ex-pected little or nothing. Safire recalled, "Bush walked right up to it, and then couldn't do it."

The president began his speech by complimenting Nixon's per-formance earlier in the day. "I think everybody across our coun-try," he said, "was once again so impressed when we saw what you did today in outlining foreign policy objectives of this country." Bush, as one politician to another, thanked Nixon for coming to Houston, Texas, and kicking off his campaign for the Senate in 1970. "I thought I was right on top of the world." Actually, Bush lost. "I am [*sic*] very, very grateful to him then." The president's tone was unnecessarily obsequious, as he continued to thank Nixon in rhythms that reminded everyone of comedian Dana Carvey's imitations of him during the 1992 campaign.

"I was grateful to him when I served—while he was President, while I was head of the Republican National Committee. And I value his advice today. I get it. I appreciate it. And I'm very grate-ful to him for his continued leadership in this area that is so vital to the United States of America."

Bush continued: "A writer once said of Richard Nixon, his life 'somehow was central to the experience of being an American in the second half of this century.' I am proud tonight to salute a President who made a difference—not because he wished it, but because he willed it."

Bush praised Nixon for his "active, thoughtful and, above all, realistic approach to the world." As president, Bush said, Nixon balanced confrontation with cooperation and managed to negoti-ate an arms control pact with the Soviet Union, an opening to China, and disengagement arrangements in the Middle East. Just as Nixon had to win domestic support for his foreign initiatives in the 1970s, so, too, did Bush in the 1990s. "We've got to find a way to square the responsibilities of world leadership with the requirements of domestic renewal."

Bush then tried to walk the thin line between agreeing with Nixon and at the same time disagreeing with him. It was not an easy feat. After all, after praising Nixon as a paragon of presidential wisdom, how could Bush criticize his vision? The president retreated to safe ground. He attacked the Buchanan themes of "protectionism" and "isolationism," assuming in advance that on this point he had Nixon's support. "There are voices across the political spectrum calling—in some cases, shouting—for America to 'come home, gut defense, spend the peace dividend, shut out foreign goods, slash foreign aid.'" Bush did not have to mention Buchanan by name. "Turning our back on the world is simply no answer. I don't care how difficult our problems are at home." Of course, that very concern was precisely why Bush's foreign policy had been muted, even partially paralyzed, throughout the campaign, but the president was also aware of Nixon's strong conviction that leadership required, as he had written in his memo, "not simply to support what is popular but to make what is unpopular popular if that serves America's national interest."

Bush recalled that, after World Wars I and II, "the United States retreated behind its oceans." With an allusion to Yeltsin's Russia, he continued: "We stood by and watched as Germany's struggling democracy, the Weimar Republic, failed under the weight of reparations, protectionism and depression, and gave way to the horror that we all know as the Third Reich." At this moment in the speech, the president could have drawn the obvious parallel to Russia and announced a major aid program for Russia. "We invested so much to win the cold war. We must invest what is necessary to win the peace. . . . We must support reform, not only in Russia, but throughout the former Soviet Union and Eastern Europe." With these words, the president walked up to the plate. "Carrying out a leadership role in determining the course of the emerging world is going to cost money." He took one pitch, and then another, and whiffed. Instead of spelling out the cost, he fell back on political rhetoric. He blamed "many in Congress" who wanted to cut defense spending. He attacked "those who would have us do less."

By this time, it was clear to everyone at the dinner that the president did not intend to "commit" news. No new Marshall Plans were to be unveiled.

Then, after patting himself on the back for his Persian Gulf victory, he concluded with a peroration about free trade, jobs, exports—all adding up to Bush's conventional wisdom: "There is no distinction between how we fare abroad and how we live at home. Foreign and domestic policy are but two sides of the same coin."

Bush then retold the story about Nixon's 1959 exchange with Nikita Khrushchev. The Soviet leader had bragged that Nixon's grandchildren would live under Communism, to which Nixon had responded, probably instinctively, that, no, it would be Khrushchev's grandchildren who would live under capitalism. It was at the time a lawyer's quick riposte, but decades later history would prove him right.

Now finished, Bush accepted the polite applause of the assembled guests and then ambled over to the head table, where he joined Nixon, Mrs. Bush, and the others. "Who's in charge here?" Bush asked. Good question. A reporter asked Nixon whether he'd support the president's reelection, even now. Of course he would, replied Nixon, the eternal Republican.

On March 12, 1992, while the conferees prepared for another day of touring the diplomatic horizon, the question of "Who lost

Russia?" was raised in many radio and television newscasts. On NBC's "Today" program, host Bryant Gumble asked Senator Nunn, just back from Moscow, whether the president was "abdicating his foreign policy responsibilities in the name of election-year politics." Searching for the right words, the senator responded: "Let me put it this way. I think the President's place in history may be determined in the next few months.... This is a unique crossroads in history. If we do not treat it as such, we will not be forgiven by future generations of Americans. Three to five years from now, the American people will say, 'Where were our leaders when we really had an opportunity to help democracy succeed in a country that will help determine the kind of world we live in for the next 20 or 30 years?'"

On ABC's "Good Morning America," Ambassador Strauss told Charles Gibson what George Bush was refusing to acknowledge to the American people—namely, that it was going to cost the United States many billions of dollars to help Russia. And the United States did not have the luxury to wait until after the election. Bush did not have the luxury, either. Strauss seemed to be struggling for a way to light a fire under the president—before it was too late, for him and for Russia. Actually, Strauss said, months before he was to quit his post in utter frustration, it was not so much a matter of helping Russia as it was a matter of helping America. "This isn't charity," he said impatiently. "This is enlightened self-interest."

On National Public Radio, reporter Anne Garrels, who covered the conference, told her listeners: "Administration officials are concerned that money thrown at Russia will be wasted. There are plenty of fights ahead over where the money is going to come from. There is a looming debate about what it means to be a superpower in this new world." Garrels accurately reflected one of the administration's muted but fundamental disagreements with

Nixon—its belief that large sums of money sent to Russia now would be lost in corruption and inefficiency.

The *New York Times,* like many other newspapers in the United States and abroad, was chock-full of Nixon stories: a Friedman analysis of the Nixon-Bush speeches, a Safire column, a Gelb column—and editors ordered up more pieces for the weekend. Radio, CNN, and the wires pumped out a stream of stories on the Nixon challenge, some of them now adding quotes from the early-morning programs. At Channel 26 in Washington and Channel 13 in New York, the co-anchors of the "MacNeil-Lehrer NewsHour" on PBS agreed early in the day that Nixon was to be their lead focus that evening. To the degree that heavy news coverage not only creates pressure but also helps shape a new political reality, the Nixon memo and conference, helped by heavy news coverage in the *New York Times,* ignited a national and international debate on the issue of aid to Russia.

"Richard Nixon's call for help is our lead story tonight," began Jim Lehrer. After a Kwame Holman set-up piece, Lehrer moderated a debate among Nunn, who seemed to spend the day hopping from one studio to another; a Republican colleague, Senator Malcolm Wallop of Wyoming; Fred Starr, president of Oberlin College in Ohio and a student of Soviet culture and society; and Professor Stephen Cohen of Princeton University, an expert on Soviet history and politics. For the first time, viewers began to see and hear a substantive discussion of the issues raised by the Nixon memo. The rhapsody of uncritical praise subsided—a bit.

Is Nixon right? asked Lehrer. "Entirely correct," replied Nunn, by now practiced in his responses. "I'm glad that he has helped focus attention. Some of us have been talking about this subject in similar terms since last September and October."

Should the United States lead a Western effort to help Russia with as much as $20 billion a year "or whatever it takes"? asked Lehrer. Senator Wallop, a staunch conservative, replied, "No, not whatever it takes." Concerned apparently that he might be putting too much distance between himself and Nixon, he added, "I do agree with President Nixon that our policy has been minimalist and might best be described as Russo-centric."

Lehrer put a political question to Fred Starr. Referring to Nixon's dark vision of a "new and more dangerous despotism" replacing Yeltsin, he asked, "Is that the way you see it?" "I don't," said Starr, who was critical of Nixon's analysis. "I think that's excessively apocalyptic. We've had various grim scenarios. None of them have come to pass. I think what his speech missed was the real sense of economic opportunity there."

Cohen was also critical of Nixon. He disagreed with the former president that it was within America's capacity to save Yeltsin and democracy—and to do both in timely fashion. "I think to formulate a policy in terms of Yeltsin is exceedingly short-sighted. Any hope for real markets or real democracy in Russia is a matter of a generation, not of one winter or five years."

Cohen warmed to his task. "I think President Nixon is wrong in saying that Russia is ours to win or lose. We can't win or lose democracy or capitalism in markets in Russia. That destiny, Russia's destiny, will be decided there by political forces." For Cohen, it was not a question of "Who lost Russia?" A country so vast was not America's to lose, any more than the United States could have lost China forty or so years before, as Nixon had earlier charged. Even with the most generous and sophisticated policy, Cohen was saying, the United States could only affect Russia's destiny "on the margins."

On March 15, 1992, Lynn Neary, host of National Public Radio's "All Things Considered," interviewed three editorial writers from different parts of the country: Lynnell Burkett of the *San Antonio Light,* Candace Page of the *Burlington Free Press,* and John Barnes of the *Detroit News.* They represented three distinct points of view. Burkett bought the Nixon approach. Like the former president, she believed that if the economic reforms in Russia failed, then "a hardline Communist leadership" would reemerge. (Nixon actually spoke of a "nationalistic" regime supplanting Yeltsin's government.) Because so few Americans were absorbed with foreign affairs, she thought that "Nixon speaking out now—he's almost given Bush cover or justification, you know, by returning to this foreign policy issue."

Page from Vermont thought very little of the Nixon memo—indeed, referred to it as "irrelevant." She said: "Richard Nixon betrayed this country, I think, and he remains unrepentant. And I'm not broadminded enough to say that that's all in the past and that we should treat the guy as a senior statesman."

Neary asked whether Page ought not to consider Nixon's expertise in foreign affairs. Page responded: "Well, you know, Leona Helmsley is an expert in hospitality, I suppose, but that doesn't mean when I'm looking for advice about how to run a hotel that she's going to be the person I choose to listen to. As I said earlier, if Richard Nixon were the only person saying this, riveting our attention on the dangers here, then perhaps it would justify attention. But he isn't. So I see the attention being paid to the man, not the message."

Barnes simply did not agree with Nixon's advice that massive aid should be dispatched to Moscow. "It is not at all clear," he said, "that foreign aid will have much effect one way or another on the course of democracy in Russia, because there isn't much of a democratic tradition there to begin with." Barnes also delved into Nixon's motivation—something few other commentators did at the time. "Mr. Nixon seems to be wanting to make a play for the history books here. He's nearly 80 years old and I think he wants to try to once again wipe out the stain of Watergate, and—and he thinks one way of doing it is playing up to a—to an establishment that seems eager to spend money to help Russia or the Soviet Union, and that seems to be what he's—what he's trying to do."

What was clear by this weekend in mid-March was that the Nixon memo and conference had generated a great deal of wide-ranging and controversial coverage about Russia, aid, foreign policy, Bush, politics, and of course the "old man" himself. And with this coverage came pressure on the president to bite the bullet on more aid to Russia, even in the midst of a reelection campaign that shunned the issue of foreign policy.

Inevitably, the storm affected the campaign. Bush's speech at the conference only reinforced the widespread impression that the White House had no vision, no program, and no voice. Jim Leach, a Republican congressman from Iowa, echoed this common view. "I think the country is crying out for leadership," he said. "When there is a major issue of our time that is not being addressed, such as the Russian aid question, the alternative party usually steps forward. This time the Democrats have not, which is why in this void the new moral voice in America is Richard Nixon." Leach, a moderate who resigned from the Foreign Service as a young man to protest Watergate, may have intended his comment to be ironic. Ironic or not, eighteen years after Watergate, Nixon was being described as "the new moral voice in America."

Looking back on the immediate aftermath of the Nixon conference, Simes told me that Nixon had always assumed that "his impact [on Bush] would be the result of his public efforts—his memo, his conference, his trips to Russia—that these would have a major impact on the Bush administration." Even if Nixon could not as yet force the president to accelerate a program of American aid to Russia, he was having an effect. His strategy was working.

"THE TIDE TURNING"

Don Oberdorfer, a few days later, returned to his journal and re-flected on the impact of the memo and the conference: "With Nixon's appearances, I could almost feel the tide turning on U.S. aid to Russia." He conferred with a number of his editors, includ-ing managing editor Robert Kaiser, who had once covered the Soviet Union for the *Washington Post,* and they all agreed that a big story was brewing. The White House was shifting its strategy, or so it seemed, from a preoccupation with domestic policy, which did not seem to be boosting the president's popularity in the polls in any case, to a greater emphasis on foreign policy, which had always been regarded as Bush's strength. The risks were obvious: foreign aid was still unpopular, and the recession was still a drag on the national economy. For the next couple of weeks, Ober-dorfer suggested, he ought to be spending all of his time covering the Russian aid question.

For Oberdorfer, Friedman, and other prominent journalists in Washington whose work bridged the worlds of diplomacy and politics, this was the big story on the near horizon—and Nixon was right in the middle of it. His role and argument raised ques-tions.

Was Nixon right? Was Western aid to Russia really necessary? How much? Which nations would provide it? What would be the American share? Even if the aid were given, could Russia absorb it? How much would be lost to sloth and corruption? Did it make sense for the West (and the United States) to rely so exclusively on Yeltsin, as it had on Gorbachev? Could Russia, with its long history of despotism, change so dramatically into a democracy and a free market economy? Would this transformation take years or decades or generations? Would Bush agree, however reluctantly, to offer the new Russia whatever amount Nixon recommended?

Like Oberdorfer, Nixon could "feel the tide turning," but he knew that there was still much work to be done. After months of intensive deliberations, he had written his memo and arranged his conference, delivered his speech, and generated a tidal wave of publicity. Now, from his office in New Jersey, he moved into the job of pure political salesmanship with characteristic doggedness and determination. He worked the phones, calling his allies on Capitol Hill, his former associates, many of whom were at the conference, and his "A" list of reporters, columnists, and op-ed page editors. He wrote short personal notes to influential people, and he planned the next steps with Simes, including another trip to Moscow. Nixon now set himself one more goal—to force the two major presidential candidates to put Russian aid at the top of their foreign policy agendas. Because he assumed at the time that Bush would win the election, Bush was his primary target.

The president felt the pressure and the need to respond to Nixon, but not to the extent that Nixon had envisaged. Bush preferred to operate in a comfort zone defined by minimalist ventures at home and dramatic but low-risk actions abroad. With respect to Russian aid, he differed with Nixon in two major respects: he believed, first, that the money would be wasted and, second, that the United States was not in a position to provide much in any case. Germany and Japan, in his view, should take the lead, but Bush had little confidence that they would be willing to do so.

Secretary Baker found himself in the awkward position of agreeing with Nixon, whom he disliked and distrusted, that the president was being much too cautious in his overall approach to the economic and political revolutions sweeping through Eastern Europe. Baker had worked very hard to manage the Middle East peace process, the defusing of the Nicaragua crisis, the disintegration of the Soviet Union, the reunification of Germany, and the shaping of the post–Cold War world, and he wanted the president to run on his achievements in foreign policy. Add the victory over Iraq during the 1991 Persian Gulf War, and Baker believed that George Bush had a strong and impressive record of accomplishment, and the American people would respect it and return him to the White House.

Even specifically on the issue of aiding Russia, Baker was of the view, which he admitted to his closest aides behind closed doors, that the United States should be giving much more. Like his former Soviet negotiating partner, Eduard Shevardnadze, who left his job as foreign minister on December 20, 1990, to become president of his native Georgia, Baker believed that the rehabilitation of Russia was a global responsibility. In January 1992, he had convened an international conference at the State Department to coordinate financial, technological, and economic assistance to Russia and other former Soviet republics. He had encouraged Bush to make a generous gesture, but the president simply refused. Nixon had derided the whole affair as a "penny ante" exercise.

Bill Clinton, by mid-March, was a candidate in deep trouble, despite the fact that he had just won a series of primaries in the South on March 10 and in Michigan and Illinois on March 17 that turned him into the presumptive nominee of the Democratic Party. He had been hounded by the press on a range of embarrassing and distracting issues, such as infidelity and draft dodging, that were generally referred to as "character questions," and he felt the need to elevate his campaign. Clinton's aides believed that it was time for a change of topic, and Nixon of all people provided the spark.

The Democratic candidate had laid out a broad vision of foreign affairs in a series of three speeches in 1991 at Georgetown University, his undergraduate alma mater, but now he was searching for a specific new theme in the area of foreign policy. "The economy, stupid!" was still to be his vehicle for victory, but his new focus was to be the product of Nixon's latest pitch: aid to Russia as a vital part of his new vision of a post–Cold War world. He told his advisers that he wanted to deliver an important speech on America's responsibilities to the new Russia on April 1 in New York. By providing a new topic of conversation for his embattled campaign, he might distract the New York tabloids from their ferocious feeding frenzy.

In any presidential campaign, plans for such a speech are naturally regarded as top secret, but in this case, the secrecy lasted no more than a few hours. When Bush learned about Clinton's idea, he quickly decided to do his own speech on Russian aid, at one and the same time making a gesture to Nixon and protecting his political flank. Not by coincidence, he chose to speak on April 1, seeking in this way to overshadow Clinton's speech and message for the day.

Nixon, meanwhile, was pressing his case on Capitol Hill, where "gridlock" had become a way of life. He knew that many members of Congress were feeling vulnerable because of criticism of their excessive perks and privileges and their meager accomplishments. Lawmakers by the dozen announced that they would not seek reelection. Nixon sensed an opportunity. In one telephone conversation after another, he put out the line that if they did not side with him, and this rare chance for democracy in Russia withered on the vine, then they would be just as vulnerable as the president to his taunting question. "Who lost Russia?"—a stick of rhetorical dynamite with huge political implications—could easily be tossed at them, too.

There was a feeling in Congress that the question of Russian aid was ripe for deliberation and perhaps even action. The week after the publication of the Nixon memo, key members of Congress met privately with Vice-President Dan Quayle and Secretary Baker. There was no ignoring the fact that Nixon's emphasis on Russian aid and his criticism of Bush had helped shape the agenda. Democrat Patrick Leahy of Vermont and Republican Richard Lugar of Indiana, working with the White House, produced a compromise between a program of generous assistance to Russia, which many in Congress preferred despite the widespread impression that foreign aid was, as Nixon put it, "poison," and one of modest but directed aid, which the White House thought would be more practical, in terms of both what Russia could absorb and what the American people would tolerate in an election year.

On March 22, the shape of an aid-to-Russia package emerged from these negotiations. The White House indicated that it could accept the package. The date was important for Bush's political calculations. Five days earlier, on March 17, the president had won decisive primary victories in Michigan and Illinois, and these effectively destroyed Buchanan's "America First" challenge from the right, which had frozen the administration's foreign policy. Now the president felt that he could again troll in foreign waters, relatively safe from conservative attack.

On March 29, Bush unveiled his plans. Speaking to reporters in Lafayette Square after attending Sunday services at St. John's Episcopal Church near the White House, he disclosed that the administration would, within a matter of days, take the wrappings off a multi-billion-dollar aid package for Russia. He provided no details. "It will be good," he said. Oberdorfer, in his *Post* article the following morning, stressed the view of several in Congress that the president would have to take the lead and fight for the package if he expected congressional approval.

On March 31, Friedman wrote in the *Times* that the administration intended the next day to propose an aid package for Russia and other countries in Eastern Europe, in effect challenging Congress to make good on its often stated aim of helping Russia. A senior official was quoted as saying: "We will be saying to Congress: 'You have been saying that we have to do more for Russia. Well, let's all hold hands together and do it.'" In this way Bush would be acting in conjunction with Congress, providing both Congress and the White House with protection against political sloganeering and criticism. Passage could conceivably come in June, after the spring recess.

When the White House was asked whether it was responding to Nixon's pressure, its answer was always no, it was planning to propose additional aid for Russia anyhow. Only once, during an appearance on "Meet the Press" on April 12, 1992, did Scowcroft grudgingly acknowledge that Nixon deserved "some credit" but "only in the sense" that he had helped elevate the policy discussion beyond the level of "just aid." On all other occasions, White House officials, including Scowcroft, usually dismissed Nixon's role.

Months later I asked Scowcroft, "What role did Nixon play in energizing the president's response?"

"None," he answered.

"None at all?"

"None."

I tried another approach. "I'm told that if it weren't for the

Nixon memo and the conference, the president wouldn't have decided to do his April 1 speech at all."

Again, Scowcroft shook his head. "We were going to do the speech anyway."

"So Nixon had no effect whatsoever on the president's policy response? His speech?"

"Look, I like the old man," Scowcroft said. "What can I say? We'd have done it without him."

On April 1, twenty-one minutes apart—Bush speaking at 11:04 A.M. at a White House news conference and Clinton at 11:25 A.M. at the Foreign Policy Association in New York—the two rivals for the presidency described their respective visions of the post–Cold War era, focusing on the matter of aid to Russia.

"We have a major stake in the success of democracy" in Russia and the other republics of the former Soviet Union, said the president, as he proposed draft legislation for a $24 billion aid package. If democratic reforms in Russia fail, Bush warned, "it could plunge us into a world more dangerous in some respects than the dark years of the Cold War." The words seemed to have been lifted, with barely a rewrite, from the Nixon memo. "The cost of doing nothing could be exorbitant," he explained. "The revolution in these states is a defining moment in history. The stakes are as high for us now as at any time in this century."

Bush claimed, "This isn't a Johnny-come-lately thing, and this isn't driven by election year politics."

The money would come, officials said, from financial institutions such as the International Monetary Fund and the World Bank and from major industrial powers such as Germany, Japan, France, Great Britain, Canada, and the United States. The $24 billion would be subdivided in the following way:

—the industrial powers would contribute $11 billion in bilateral aid, including commodity credits and general and humanitarian aid, with $2.6 billion coming from the United States;

—the IMF and the World Bank would provide $4.5 billion, with $900 million coming from the United States;

—$2.5 billion in foreign debt would be rescheduled, none of it by the United States;

—a $6 billion fund for ruble stabilization would be established, with $1.5 billion coming from the United States.

The total would be $24 billion, of which the contribution of the United States would be $5 billion.

Twenty-four billion dollars sounded like a lot of money, a head-line-catching proposal that seemed to respond to the Nixon/Yeltsin challenge. It suggested boldness in foreign policy, which is what Bush wanted to convey. But it quickly became clear that the plan was both vague and hastily conceived. The White House told reporters that it had been coordinated with America's allies, but the allies denied it. Chancellor Helmut Kohl of Germany was the first to question not only the total amount but the dates of delivery. Japan took the unusual step of publicly criticizing the United States and labeling Bush's "rush" to philanthropy "inappropriate" and "premature." In any case, Tokyo insisted, there had been no agreement on the total amount or the breakdown. "It's larger than the size we were told of," said the vice-minister of finance, Hiroshi Yasuda. "About $6 billion larger," he added (*Chicago Tribune,* April 5, 1992).

Clinton knew that by challenging Bush on foreign policy, he started at a considerable disadvantage. *USA Today* and CNN/Gallup had just published a poll stating that only 22 percent of the

American people felt that he could do a good job in the areas of foreign and defense policies, while 70 percent thought that Bush was better equipped to handle these responsibilities.

In a bid to reverse these figures, Clinton went on the offensive. He described the president's overall foreign policy as "reactive, rudderless and erratic" (Jessica Lee, *USA Today,* April 2, 1992, p. 1A) and contrasted it with his own broader vision of a foreign policy based on democracy and human rights.

When it came to the specific issue of aid to Russia, Clinton's proposal was remarkably similar to the president's. He, too, supported the general proposition that the Western industrialized nations should help Russia transform itself from a Communist dictatorship to a free market democracy. But Clinton used the Nixon memo to embarrass Bush. "Prodded by Democrats in Congress, rebuked by Richard Nixon, and realizing that I have been raising the issue in the campaign, the President is finally . . . putting forward a plan," he said.

The "Bush-Clinton Debate," in columnist Safire's words, led the newscasts on April 1 and dominated newspaper headlines on April 2. "Bush and Kohl Unveil Plan for 7 Nations to Contribute $24 Billion in Aid for Russia," said the *New York Times.* A subheadline read, "Buying Time for Yeltsin." Friedman covered Clinton's slashing attack on Bush. The president, according to Clinton, "failed to provide a compelling vision to justify American engagement abroad after the cold war." Safire compared the two speeches and concluded that "Clinton came out standing a little taller." The headline in the *Boston Globe* story read, "Clinton Criticizes Bush's Foreign Policy as Overly 'Passive.'" The *Wall Street Journal* featured only the president: "Bush, Allies Pledge $24 Billion to Russia." *Time* columnist Michael Kramer credited Nixon with prodding Bush to advance a plan to help Russia. "Bush was mute," he wrote, "until Richard Nixon chastised the President for a 'pathetically inadequate' nonresponse to Moscow's pleas for help" (Kramer, *Time*, April 13, 1992, p. 28).

When the two speeches were compared, it was clear that Bush remained a president on the defensive. "It's not a tremendous amount of money," he said at one point in a gesture toward voters who objected to helping a former enemy; and then moments later, in a strained response to critics, such as Nixon and Clinton, he continued, "Our commitment is very, very substantial."

The president wanted to have his cake and eat it too. His program of aid to Russia fell short of what Nixon proposed but went too far for his critics. It also posed problems in connection with institutional loans. IMF and World Bank credit terms were so stringent that it was doubtful Yeltsin could meet them. In order to present a proper balance sheet to these international institutions, Yeltsin would have to raise taxes and prices, tighten internal credit, reduce imports, and slash social programs. Such austerity, if seriously implemented, might well undercut his political viability.

Boris Khorev, an economist at Moscow State University, voiced the Kremlin's concerns. "We're not against help," he said, "but we won't accept the dictatorship of the IMF." Ironically, conservatives in the United States agreed. Robert Bartley of the *Wall Street Journal*'s editorial page argued against "delivering the Russians to the tender mercies of experts at the IMF." Buchanan, still an active candidate though his political wings had been clipped, told CNN's Larry King that the Bush aid package was only intended to cover bad German loans to Russia. "This is a big Ponzi scheme," he said, describing IMF-style reform as "the Lincoln S&L of the new world order."

Nevertheless, with all its faults, the Bush administration did present an aid package for Russia and, to a significant extent, this was the result of Nixon's pressure. True, a number of senior senators, led by Nunn, Lugar, and Bill Bradley, had for some months been pushing for a major aid program for Russia. But it was Nixon's memo that focused attention on the issue.

In the immediate aftermath of the April 1 speeches, Nixon again dominated conversation at Washington dinner parties. What was Nixon's game? Was he genuinely interested in aiding Russia, a country he had detested for most of his political life? Or was Russia a hobby seized upon for his amusement in the twilight of his life? Or was it simply a case of Nixon's pouncing on any available initiative that could advance his rehabilitation?

Many who knew Nixon only as a historical figure have concluded that late in his life he became a selfless politician, a Good Samaritan eager to help his fellow citizens of the world. It would be ungenerous to suggest that Nixon did not want to aid Russia at this pivotal moment in world history, but it would be naive in the extreme to ignore his central motivation. Those who knew Nixon well, who served him loyally or observed him dispassionately for decades, have never abandoned their basic view of the man—that Nixon always thought about Nixon first and everything else second. A number of them have come to believe that Simes persuaded Nixon of the importance of the question of helping Russia and that Nixon then seized on it as the perfect, proper, and respectable cause to advance his deeper purposes of personal rehabilitation. "There's lots of reason," said one former Nixon adviser, "to be skeptical about his motivation." There was never any doubt in the minds of those closest to the former president that if Nixon had to choose between rehabilitation of himself and the rescue of Russia, he would, to quote columnist Safire, embrace rehabilitation "without a moment's hesitation."

Nixon envisaged struggle as a constant companion and life as an eternal battle. He felt that he had no choice but to fight his political enemies—to outsmart and outmaneuver and outwork them. Watergate, the great divide in his life, was to him a grotesquely unfair episode, and, by whatever means, he was determined to recover his place in history.

He once told columnist Roger Rosenblatt: "Renewal. Americans are crazy about renewal" (Rosenblatt, *Time,* April 25, 1988, p. 54). Rosenblatt concluded after a number of interviews that Nixon enjoyed spinning the globe, studying the swift and fascinating patterns of politics and diplomacy, and then, in books and interviews, offering his insights into elections, revolutions, and wars. But there was more. Nixon felt that many Americans wanted to see him fall but then get up from the floor and fight again. This "graceless, awkward, stiff, stumbling character," to quote Rosenblatt, found that there was always an audience for a story about a politician who bounced back from adversity, always a journalist ready to be attracted by his tale of controversy and resilience.

Alexander Haig, who was his chief of staff during Watergate and later, in 1988, ran for president, told me, "I would have bet a million dollars that Nixon would have blown his rehabilitation." But through a "carefully orchestrated" process, Nixon moved relentlessly toward his goal. Nothing distracted him. Though he suffered "terribly," Haig said, Nixon remained "fully engaged" in foreign affairs, a magnet for many Republicans and others "who admired his toughness."

* * *

National Public Radio, usually sober in its presentation of the news, was struck by the fact that Bush and Clinton had both delivered their speeches on April 1—April Fool's Day. The afternoon program "Talk of the Nation" invited Rich Little to do one of his famous Richard Nixon impersonations on air. "Having marched up this hard road and won back your confidence," Little/Nixon pronounced, "I ask you once again to make me your President." The phones "went berserk," said an NPR spokesperson, obliging the network to confess that it was all a joke.

CHAPTER

10

THE ULTIMATE IRONY

Two months later, Nixon was back in Moscow, aware that the $24 billion aid package, launched with such fanfare on April 1, was languishing on Capitol Hill. He was a man with a mission, even though he held no official appointment. When he met with Yeltsin on June 4, 1992, they spoke of the possibility—indeed, the likelihood—that Russia was dangerously close to social and economic collapse. They envisaged a city or a region exploding into violence, people taking to the streets in anger and frustration at the lack of food, shelter, and hope.

Without any authority from the U.S. government, without even the courtesy of a nod toward the U.S. ambassador in Moscow, Nixon reached broad agreement with Yeltsin on an extraordinary arrangement for American help to Russia in the event of an emergency. Yeltsin must have believed that Nixon, a former president, was speaking on behalf of his government. Simes negotiated what he later called "the technical details" with one of Yeltsin's foreign policy advisers, and in Washington Russian Ambassador Lukin was kept informed of this highly irregular negotiation. These were the terms, as described by Simes: Nixon would, on his return to the United States, contact twenty or more CEOs of leading American corporations for pledges of immediate aid to Russia—food, blankets, medical supplies, transportation. Then, when and if the news of rioting in a major Russian city filled the TV screens, signaling a full-blown international crisis, U.S. government transport planes would fly the aid to the scene of the trouble. Hopefully, this would save Russian lives and salvage Yeltsin's position.

Officially, the U.S. government knew nothing about this plan. When Baker was finally informed, he checked with Bush and, on instruction, sent a deliberately vague message to Nixon. It represented neither a yes nor a no. Would U.S. transport planes be allowed to fly the emergency aid to Russia? They did not say. Neither Baker nor Bush wanted to antagonize Nixon in the midst of the presidential campaign; nor did they wish to encourage his meddling in sensitive diplomatic matters. The White House reaction, in other words, was most decidedly half-hearted.

By contrast, during Nixon's next meeting with Yeltsin, on February 10, 1993, soon after Clinton took office, a totally different kind of discussion took place. From their common concern about imminent violence, which had not materialized, they now shifted to the subject of long-range economic and political assistance. Yeltsin proudly informed Nixon that what he had feared most had not happened—there had not been a single strike during the bitter winter of 1992–93. The people were exhausted, inflation was dreadful, and the gridlock with parliament was paralyzing, but there had been no social upheaval. In a land of minimal expectations, Yeltsin thought that was at least a step in the right direction and deserved recognition.

Nixon agreed with Yeltsin but argued for realism. Large-scale government-to-government aid was unlikely. Germany was preoccupied with the reconstruction of its eastern provinces, once under Communist control. Japan was obsessed with the Kurile Islands and seemed to condition aid on their return. The United States, under a new administration, was determined to focus on its own economic recovery. Nixon had high hopes for private foreign investment in Russia, citing projections as high as $700 billion over the next four to five years, but not until Yeltsin set up the constitutional and legal underpinning for such a major financial commitment.

In the meantime, Nixon proposed a different approach. He advanced the idea of targeted aid—a series of specific projects that would sidestep the largely corrupt Moscow bureaucracy and send assistance directly to the Russian people. He cited a number of examples, such as the establishment of an entrepreneurial fund to help Russians set up small- to medium-sized businesses, dispatching Peace Corps and agricultural volunteers, arranging loan guarantees to build homes for displaced Soviet troops, and, most important, rescheduling Russia's huge $84 billion foreign debt for fifteen years.

Nixon stressed that such a broad package of assistance would require U.S. leadership and courage and a strong personal commitment from President Clinton, who had promised the American people that he would focus like a "laser beam" on the domestic economy and not get entangled in foreign affairs. Nixon promised Yeltsin that he would now uncork all of his formidable talents to persuade the press and the new Clinton administration to adopt his program.

Nixon started by giving an exclusive interview to Serge Schmemann, the *New York Times*'s bureau chief in Moscow. It was Nixon's way of communicating with the power elites in Washington, Moscow, and other world capitals. Accompanied by a photograph of Nixon gazing into the distance, the story appeared on page 4, February 19, 1993, under the headline, "Who'll Speak Up for Russia Now? Nixon, No Less." "I'm an anti-Communist," he told Schmemann, "but a pro-Russian." The anti-and-pro combination was typical of Nixon's skill at shaping a reporter's story.

"Old cold warriors need not fade away," Schmemann began.

"Take Richard M. Nixon—at 80, he is battling on with much of the same fervor he showed in his celebrated jousts with Nikita S. Khrushchev 34 years ago. Only he is not fighting against Communists now, but for Russia."

In the interview, Nixon test-marketed a series of phrases and ideas that he would use on his return to the United States with other journalists, columnists, scholars, entrepreneurs—and, most important, with President Bill Clinton.

They were:

—The new Russia is a "democracy." Instead of Russia exporting Communism, Nixon said, "it will be exporting freedom to the world," proof for the developing nations that the Russian model made more sense for them than the Chinese model of economic reform constrained by political repression.

—Boris Yeltsin is a "strong, very strong" leader.

—The Russian economic collapse of the 1990s is much worse than the American depression of the 1930s. "How any government could still go forward with reforms is just amazing."

—According to the latest Gallup Poll, only 4 percent of the American people care about foreign policy. "Last week," Nixon told Schmemann, "we had another example—Clinton appeared on a town meeting in Michigan, a national town meeting, where he took questions, no holds barred. There was only one question about foreign policy—it was about Bosnia, not about Russia at all."

—Clinton must lead the charge for Russian aid. "It's the responsibility of a leader to educate the people so they will support what needs to be done. Putting it more simply, you don't take people where they want to go, you take people where they ought to go." Nixon had urged Bush to do the same thing the year before.

—Foreign and domestic policy are like Siamese twins: "separate them," Nixon said, "and they die."

—Russian pride must be respected. "Today they're being treated as a second-rate power. . . . One of the things that is absolutely essential is that we not consider Russia to be a defeated enemy."

The next obvious step was to arrange a White House meeting with the president. Ever since Clinton's election in November 1992, Nixon had been trying to see Clinton and ingratiate himself with the new administration. He realized that it would not be easy. Nixon and Clinton were poles apart in experience, in outlook, and in ideology. Nixon was a Cold War Republican, Clinton a baby-boomer Democrat. Nixon expanded the American war in Southeast Asia, Clinton marched in protest against it. Nixon personified Watergate, Clinton's wife had worked for Nixon's impeachment on the staff of the House Judiciary Committee. Still, Nixon wrote Clinton a long, substantive, and thoughtful letter of congratulations, and in a November 19, 1992, op-ed piece in the *New York Times,* he praised Clinton for "aggressively addressing a number of important issues during the transition period."

But if Nixon expected a quick response, he was to be disappointed. He tried to figure out who or what was the obstacle. Finally, he settled on Hillary Rodham Clinton. Roger Stone, who had been using all his Republican and Democratic contacts to help Nixon arrange a meeting, told me, "Nixon blamed Hillary." According to Stone, Nixon described Mrs. Clinton as "what we used to call a 'red-hot' in the 1930s—a real lefty like Eleanor Roosevelt" (*New York Times,* April 25, 1994, p. B8).

Shortly before Clinton's inauguration, in mid-January 1993, Nixon resumed his effort to make an impact on the president-elect. He got Stone to send an "urgent" message to Clinton— that the situation in Russia was "very grave" and that Clinton was not getting the "straight story" from the State Department, principally, Nixon said, because Baker was a roadblock. Again, there was no response from Clinton or any of his aides.

Immediately after the inauguration, Nixon, undaunted, sent another "urgent" message to Clinton. This time Stone used Richard Morris, a pollster from Arkansas, as his intermediary. Stone told me that the Nixon message contained three points and what can only be construed as a whiff of political blackmail. First, Stone said that Clinton would find Nixon's perspective on Russia to be "valuable." Second, a Nixon-Clinton meeting would "buy" the president a "one-year moratorium" on Nixon criticism of his policy toward Bosnia and other matters. And third, a Clinton-Nixon meeting would generate Republican support for aid to Russia and possibly for a budget compromise on Capitol Hill. Stone continued, "Morris told the Clintons that if Nixon was received at the White House, he couldn't come back and kick you in the teeth."

A few days later, on the eve of Nixon's February 1993 visit to Moscow, according to Stone, Morris called him and said that Clinton had agreed in principle to a meeting with Nixon, but no date had been set. Another week passed. Nixon, in Moscow, had met with Yeltsin and promised action. Stone called James Carville and Paul Begala, two of Clinton's closest political advisers, and urged that a date be fixed, especially since now Clinton could also benefit from a Nixon briefing on his meeting with Yeltsin. Begala immediately saw the political advantages of a meeting. In his mind there was no point in antagonizing Nixon, not when so much of the Clinton program rode on a degree of GOP cooperation on Capitol Hill.

Prodded by Stone, Begala rode herd on the matter of the meeting. He told John Podesta, who managed the traffic flow into the Oval Office, to make certain that the three-point Nixon message reached the president's desk. "You really ought to call him," Begala advised. Yes, Clinton agreed, but again nothing happened.

When Nixon returned from Moscow, determined to help Yeltsin but still with no date set for a meeting with Clinton, he intensified his efforts. From his New Jersey office, lined with photographs of Nixon with world leaders from another era, the former president immediately went back to one of his most productive pastimes—working the phones. He called, among others, Robert Strauss, who had recently resigned as U.S. ambassador to Russia, and Bob Dole, who as Senate Minority Leader had become the most prominent Republican in Washington after Bush's defeat. Nixon seeded his conversations with insider tidbits and fascinating gossip about Kremlin politics and then sketched a picture of almost certain catastrophe unless the West opened a pipeline of aid. He made a very compelling case. Within hours, the bipartisan team of Strauss and Dole called the White House and urged the president to meet with Nixon.

At the same time, the former president told Simes, who had accompanied Nixon to Moscow, to contact Simes's friends in the administration and inform them of the "novelty" of Nixon's concept of short-term, targeted aid. Simes called Talbott, then Clinton's point man on Russia. Would *he* want to see Nixon? Would *the president* want to see Nixon? Anthony Lake, the president's national security adviser, was also briefed on the Nixon-Yeltsin talk. Would it not make sense to discuss aid with Nixon before the administration finalized its policy on this important subject?

For his part, as days passed with no call from the White House, an increasingly frustrated Stone encouraged Nixon to "bludgeon" Clinton in much the same way as he had Bush. During the Vietnam War, as president, Nixon had employed a tactic that French journalist Michel Tatu labeled "credible irrationality," Nixon's way of frightening the North Vietnamese into believing that he would be capable of doing anything to achieve his ends and they had better be accommodating. In this spirit he let Stone spread the word in Washington that he was losing his patience. Stone called Tony Coelho, a former Democratic congressman from California with superb contacts at the White House, and warned that Nixon was on the edge of exploding. The situation in Russia was desperate. Nixon had ideas—and a short fuse. Could Coelho help arrange a Nixon meeting with Clinton? The implication was clear: a meeting would buy time, information, and maybe cooperation; further delay would buy upheaval in Russia and political confrontation at home.

Nixon also sniffed the political and journalistic winds and figured that, along with the private pressure, it was time for him to go public again. He decided that another "shot across the bow," as Stone put it, was now in order. It was to be a warning shot at the new administration that Nixon had to be recognized as a player in policy deliberations on Russia and Yeltsin. Once again, the shot was to be fired from the op-ed page of the *New York Times*. Stone later recalled warning his White House contacts that the "piece could be gentle or not so gentle" ("CBS Evening News," April 27, 1994, interview with Rita Braver).

A Nixon aide phoned Levitas, editor of the op-ed page, to ask whether the *Times* would be interested in another long Nixon piece on aid to Russia. Levitas responded with alacrity, as he had on several other occasions over the past year. Not only had Levitas published Schorr's piece about the Nixon memo on March 10,

1992, but then twice in five months (June 12, 1992, and November 19, 1992) he had run other pieces by Nixon about aid to Russia, and here he was, three months later, ready to run yet another Nixon piece on the same subject. There is a policy at the *Times* that no writer should be published more than once in six months on the op-ed page. Obviously, at the editor's discretion, that policy can be waived.

In this case, rather than draft an angry "Who lost Russia?" attack on Clinton's policy toward Russia, Nixon surprisingly drafted the political equivalent of a love letter to the new president. His reasoning seemed to be that Clinton's policy had not yet been formed and there was still a chance that Clinton could be persuaded to follow his recommendations. It did not take a Nixonologist to read his warning between the lines. If Clinton did not see him and did not follow his policy, Nixon would go on the attack. The "moratorium" that he had offered to the president in his three-point message would be null and void.

"Those who disagree, as I do, with some of the specific proposals in President Clinton's economic program," he began, "must give him credit for his boldness and political courage in advocating them and for his indefatigable efforts to sell them to the American people." Nixon continued: "If he demonstrates the same leadership qualities in addressing the major foreign policy issue of our time, he can secure his place in history as a great President. That issue is the survival and success of political and economic freedom in Russia." Nixon closed his piece on the same note. He asserted that if Clinton adopted his program of aiding Russia, "by leading abroad as he has so effectively at home, President Clinton will establish himself as the world's pre-eminent statesman."

Nixon's specific recommendations, as drafted and published, were few and familiar. Western aid to Russia was essential. Nixon urged the president to summon an emergency meeting of the Group of Seven, the leaders of the major industrialized nations. The G-7 should deliver on its promised $24 billion aid package and then reschedule Russia's $84 billion foreign debt. Germany and Japan should significantly increase their aid to Russia.

Scattered throughout Nixon's draft were questionable observations about Russia:

—"Russian workers are among the best in the world."
—"President Yeltsin shares our values."
—"Russia did not lose the cold war, the Communists did."

Nixon used the same words, phrases, and sentences he had earlier tried out on Schmemann:

—"Without a substantial increase in aid from the West, the Yeltsin government will not survive."
—"The last Gallup poll showed that only 4% of voters considered foreign policy to be an important issue."
—"In Mr. Clinton's nationally televised town meeting, there was only one question concerning foreign policy. It was about Bosnia."
—"Russia is going through an economic downturn worse than the Great Depression of the 1930's in the United States."
—"Foreign and domestic policy are like Siamese twins—one cannot survive without the other."

Levitas had to have known that these were not original policy recommendations conceived especially for this op-ed submission. They had been under consideration in academic and governmental circles for more than a year, and they were not unfamiliar to *Times* readers. Still, to Levitas, they had the ring of authenticity and urgency; the author was Nixon, and Levitas wanted to ride this story. Once again the *Times* was to be the vehicle for the

Nixon message. The fact that it reflected the paper's own editorial position was not really relevant; Levitas operated with editorial independence.

At 9:40 P.M. on March 3, 1993—the day Levitas and his staff were editing Nixon's draft for March 5 publication—Clinton picked up his phone and asked the White House operator to get Richard Nixon. Whatever might have been Clinton's earlier reservations about a meeting, including Mrs. Clinton's strong objections, he shelved them. When the operator found the former president at his residence in New Jersey, for a moment she could not find the president. "I'll wait," Nixon said, easing the embarrassment. "He's a helluva lot busier than I am." (Nixon later told Simes that he was "totally surprised" by the Clinton call.)

They spoke for forty minutes and agreed to meet on March 8, 1993, at the White House. Nixon was, an impressed Clinton later told an adviser, "full of useful information." The deal was that Nixon would enter and leave by the back door. No cameras. No press. There would be a record, however. The official White House photographer would be allowed to take a few shots but not for immediate release to the press. On March 21, 1993, one finally appeared—you guessed it!—in the *New York Times,* as a result of an exclusive arrangement between George Stephanopoulos, then White House communications director, and R. W. Apple, Jr., the Washington bureau chief. A few days later, Stephanopoulos told reporters that President Clinton wanted Nixon's "impressions of the state of the Russian economy and his specific ideas on what the United States and its allies might do to help Russia at this time."

While accurate, the Stephanopoulos explanation was incomplete. It was plain that Nixon was not in Clinton's pantheon of political heroes. But he had decided to receive Nixon in the White House anyway. Why? Was it just a touch of Southern politeness, or a shrewd political calculation? Would a meeting actually "buy" a "moratorium" on Nixon's criticism of Clinton's foreign policy? Or was Clinton, as were so many others in Washington, bewitched by Nixon's self-crafted image as an "elder statesman"—wise and experienced, the newest Nixon endowed with insights and knowledge few others possessed? Was it possible, as a number of Clinton's advisers later maintained, that Clinton never even took Vietnam and Watergate into account? When asked why Clinton would want to associate himself with the only president forced to resign in disgrace, Begala responded that Nixon had "an amazing political mind that really understands America and foreign policy" and he ought "to be listened to."

The most likely explanation was that Clinton, concerned about his own comparative inexperience in matters of foreign affairs and national security, decided that it would be wiser to engage Nixon than to isolate him. Stephanopoulos, eleven years old at the time of the Watergate scandal, later told a friend that he thought the idea of a Clinton-Nixon meeting was "wonderful." Like others in the White House, both his age and older, Stephanopoulos seemed utterly tone deaf to the inappropriateness of a Democratic president treating Nixon as a revered foreign policy adviser.

On March 5, 1993, Nixon's op-ed piece appeared in the *Times* and Clinton announced that he would meet Yeltsin at a summit in Vancouver, Canada, on April 3–4. At the same time the president would try to persuade his colleagues in the G-7 to help Russia strengthen democratic and economic reform. "I don't want to make any sweeping commitments," he told reporters, "but I'm going there to this meeting with the intention of trying to more aggressively engage the United States in the economic and political revitalization of Russia." Had Nixon's op-ed piece influenced his decision? Yes, the president said. He agreed with its "general thrust."

Nixon had promised Yeltsin that he would try to persuade Clinton to help Russia. It appeared that he had succeeded. In addition, his op-ed piece in the *Times* provided the Washington press corps with an up-to-date record of Nixon's views. When reporters wrote about the upcoming Vancouver summit, they also wrote about Nixon's views. When diplomats reported to their capitals about the summit, they also wrote about Nixon. One dovetailed with the other.

For Nixon, payoff day at the White House came on Monday, March 8, 1993. Earlier that day Clinton had consulted with his predecessor, George Bush, for the first time since the election. They discussed American options on Russia. There was no indication that Bush offered any new ideas.

To quote from Friedman's front-page story in the *Times* the following morning, "As political odd couples go, Bill Clinton and Richard Nixon surely rank with the oddest." White House staffers, many in their twenties and thirties, for whom Nixon was a figure out of their American history books, waited expectantly to catch a glimpse of the former president. Nixon, the story noted, generated as much interest and curiosity as the Dallas Cowboys, who had visited the White House the week before. "Everyone was intrigued," said one White House official. "It came up at the staff meeting this morning. People just said: 'Can you believe this? Nixon's coming.' But the fact is, he has something to offer."

The president and the former president met in the family quarters, and they spoke for about an hour, longer than either had planned. No aides were present. All accounts of the meeting were secondhand. According to a Nixon partisan who was briefed afterwards, Clinton, always the gracious host, complimented Nixon on his op-ed piece in the *Times,* and Nixon, always the carefully prepared lawyer, moved quickly into a point-by-point tour of the Russian horizon. It paralleled many of the points he had earlier made in the Schmemann interview and in the op-ed piece in the *Times*.

To begin with, Nixon said, playing to Clinton's partisanship, the Bush administration had not done enough to help Yeltsin. When Bush finally agreed to provide aid, it was not focused, much of it was wasted, and billions never even reached Russia. Nixon emphasized that only Clinton could sell the aid package to Congress. Control of the aid package must be taken out of the hands of the IMF—"too inefficient and too inflexible," Nixon said. Control must be given to the G-7 industrialized nations. Though government-to-government aid was urgently needed, ultimately only private investment could save Russia. Nixon suggested an idea for emergency assistance, strikingly similar to the one he had concocted with Yeltsin in June 1992—that Clinton convene a conference of the top one hundred corporate giants in America and, with offers of new credit and tax incentives, lobby them for new investments in Russia. As he had promised Yeltsin he would tell Clinton, Nixon stressed that aid had to be targeted; for example, the West should undertake to improve the efficiency of Russia's natural gas pipeline to Western Europe. When completed, the pipeline would provide gas to the West and profits and jobs for Russians.

Finally, Nixon returned obliquely to the question of "Who lost Russia?" which he had first raised in his memo of March 1992. He reminded Clinton that recent American presidents had been plagued by foreign policy failures that ultimately destroyed their places in history. He said that he and Johnson had been crippled by Vietnam, and Carter by the Iran hostage crisis. He warned Clinton that Russia could destroy his administration's legacy unless he acted with speed and courage. The implication was that if Clinton continued to follow "the Nixon line" on aid to Yeltsin and Russia, he could achieve greatness. On the other hand, if, like

Bush, Clinton crumbled before the obvious challenge, then he and his administration would fail and he would be a one-term president.

Throughout their meeting, Nixon did most of the talking, Clinton the listening. The politician in Clinton appreciated the commitment in Nixon. Both were accomplished pros. They parted with a warm handshake. A week later, Clinton told a friend that he was going to do everything in his power to help Russia (R. W. Apple, Jr., *New York Times,* March 24, 1993, p. 10). It would be better, he said, to try and fail than, to quote Apple, "to sit on his hands and allow his critics to accuse him of having passively lost Russia, as Harry S. Truman's enemies for so many years accused him of having 'lost' China." And who led those critics in their condemnation of Truman's China policy? Who first raised the question of "Who lost China"? The very same visitor who was now hanging the question of "Who lost Russia?" over another Democratic president.

Clinton was pragmatic about Nixon. If he was going to provide aid to Russia, as he intended in any case, then he would need help, especially on Capitol Hill, and he was ready to accept it from anyone. The president asked Nixon if he could try to drum up support among conservative Democratic and Republican senators, a job Nixon accepted with pleasure. He had intended to stay in Washington anyway for Strom Thurmond's ninetieth birthday party the following evening and for a private meeting with Strobe Talbott; now he had, in addition, a presidential assignment.

The meeting with Clinton catapulted Nixon back into the center of Washington's politics, into the good graces not only of Republicans but also of Democrats. "God, what a comeback! Who'd have believed it possible?" Such was the reaction of Stephen Ambrose, one of Nixon's many biographers, who was director of the

Eisenhower Center at the University of New Orleans. "There he was, back on the front page, making policy." Just as Bush and Reagan had consulted with Nixon before their summits with the Russians, so Clinton was now conferring with Nixon before the Vancouver summit. "It could have been done quietly, like Bush and Reagan did," said Ambrose. "But Clinton sees advantages in having Mr. Cold Warrior on his side" (John Broder, *Los Angeles Times,* March 10, 1993, p. 13).

The following day, March 9, 1993, during a meeting with senators on Capitol Hill, Nixon gave his imprimatur, for the record, to Clinton's policy of aiding Russia. At some time in the future, differences between Clinton and Nixon were almost certain to arise, but now Nixon had a president in his corner and he could not have been more pleased. For one of the president's closest political aides, this was also a moment to savor but for different reasons. "Now," this White House official crowed, without any embarrassment about Watergate, "we have Nixon's stamp of approval. Now we have the old guard Republican establishment in our corner. That's big stuff for a kid from Little Rock. I know Nixon is a disgraced president, but, in both reality and perception, he has a powerful voice in foreign affairs. He's been on the cutting edge of U.S.–Russian relations for 50 years, and now he's our spokesman on the Hill." He paused. "This is a mutually beneficial arrangement."

Nixon did his job in high style, using a Democratic president's name and credibility to advance his own ideas about aiding Russia. Nixon praised the president's foresight and wisdom, especially his "courageous leadership" in pointing the American people in a direction they had little interest in taking. Polls showed a clear majority of Americans opposed to large-scale aid to Russia. A CNN/ *USA Today* poll put the figure at 80 percent. A *New York Times/* CBS News poll put it, more conservatively, at 51 percent.

While Nixon sold his aid message on Capitol Hill, Clinton briefed visiting French President François Mitterand at the White House. When a reporter asked about his meeting with Nixon, Clinton smiled. "Great," he replied. "We were pretty much on the same wavelength, and we have been pretty much on the same wavelength on this issue for more than a year now. . . . He gave me a lot of very good ideas."

From Moscow came word of high-level appreciation of Nixon's efforts. Foreign Minister Andrei Kozyrev, no doubt reflecting Yeltsin's views, told Schmemann of the *Times* that he perceived a "shift of public debate in the United States," and he credited Nixon with this "positive development" (Serge Schmemann, *New York Times,* March 9, 1993, p. 7). After many months of promises, rarely fulfilled, the United States seemed on the edge of a major national commitment.

For his part, Nixon continued to cooperate with the president. In response to an idea advanced by Democratic Senator Alan Cranston, Nixon joined the other three living Republican ex-presidents—Ford, Reagan, and Bush—and sent a flattering letter to Clinton praising his "commitment to help sustain and develop democracy and free market reforms" in the former Soviet Union. "In keeping with the best traditions of bipartisanship in American foreign policy," they wrote, "unless we take action now to help the reformers in the successor states [of the former Soviet Union], we are likely to find any peace dividend short-lived and to face a world conceivably as dangerous and threatening to us as what we faced before." This letter, which reflected the Nixon line and which the White House promptly released to the press, was designed to protect Clinton from congressional criticism as he embarked on an uncertain journey to the Vancouver summit.

On March 26, 1993, Nixon gave an interview to Hugh Sidey of *Time*. Between the lines there was a message for Clinton: if you fail to meet the many challenges of aiding Russia, then you will pay a heavy political price. A drastically edited version of the interview appeared in the April 5, 1993, issue of *Time*. It was twinned with another interview, which reporter Christopher Ogden did with Mikhail Gorbachev in Canada. Captioned "Advice from Two Old Pros," both interviews appeared on page 27 under a picture of Gorbachev receiving Nixon in the Kremlin in 1991, when he was still in power.

Nixon, mixing kind words with clear warnings, said: "I think Clinton is making a gutsy call, really the mark of a leader. There's no question a majority of the American people at this time would oppose aid to Russia. Clinton realizes that if the Yeltsin government goes down, it means the peace dividend is down the tube and the defense budget has to be increased by billions of dollars." As for Yeltsin, Nixon argued: "Without our help, [he] will certainly fail. The choice we have here is between Yeltsin with his weaknesses and an alternative. Having met all the players, I can say there's not one of them that would not be worse." And, finally, on Western aid he said: "It has to be substantially more than has currently been discussed. We must avoid doing just enough to get our feet wet, but not enough to work. If we're not prepared to do the whole job, then we should stay out of it."

What was fascinating was that the president and his stable of young advisers failed to pick up the warning signal. They were still enchanted by the idea that Richard Nixon was supporting Bill Clinton. They did not consider the other side of the coin—that Bill Clinton was supporting Richard Nixon. Roger Stone and Paul Begala found themselves kidding each other about whether they should start up a "Friends of Bill and Dick" club. One day, a

White House aide tossed a copy of *Time* on a columnist's desk. "Read what Nixon said about Clinton?" he asked. When the columnist later read the interview, he called the adviser and asked whether anyone at the White House had read the *whole* interview? "Who do you think Nixon had in mind when he says if we're not prepared to do the whole job, we shouldn't do any of it?"

In preparation for the Vancouver summit, Clinton delved through mountains of position papers, looking for a way to help Russia without having to come up with new money. He urged his aides to be "bold," but in fact they were obliged to be cautious. For reasons ranging from strict regulations imposed by the International Monetary Fund to bureaucratic chaos in Russia, less than half of the money had actually been delivered, much of it in grain credits, which helped feed the Russian people but also increased Russia's foreign debt.

Vancouver proved to be an exceptional summit. The leaders of the United States and Russia met not as acknowledged adversaries but as potential partners. No longer was arms control the central theme at a summit; now it was the new subject of economics— more specifically, aid to Russia. Clinton seemed determined to help Yeltsin in every way—treating him as an equal, praising him as a "democrat" and as a "reformer," and promising his fragile regime a $1.6 billion U.S. aid package. That the package was composed of totally "old" money did little to lessen Clinton's optimism or Yeltsin's expressions of gratitude. Reporting on the Vancouver summit, Secretary of State Warren Christopher said that Yeltsin was "the best exponent—indeed, the only exponent of the policies that we care about" ("MacNeil-Lehrer NewsHour," April 5, 1993).

In Washington and Moscow, it had by now become the accepted wisdom among many policymakers that Nixon was right: it was America's special responsibility at this crossroads in history to help Russia shake off the repressive legacy of Communism by contributing substantial economic assistance to its former adversary. The ultimate irony was that Nixon had a greater impact on Democrat Bill Clinton than he had had on Republican George Bush.

11

SHADOW MINISTER

For the last year of his life, Richard Nixon served as a kind of shadow minister for Russian affairs in the Clinton administration. According to one White House official, Clinton "admired him enormously," especially "his ability to conceptualize complex issues." According to a senior State Department official, the president believed that he faced problems concerning post-Communist Russia similar to those Nixon had faced twenty years earlier during the period of détente and that he had much to learn from Nixon's experience. When a major problem or challenge arose in U.S.–Russian relations, Clinton would on occasion call Nixon or Nixon would write a private memo to the president.

More routinely, they maintained contact through two of their most trusted aides: Dimitri Simes, who had become Nixon's unofficial chief of staff and, for his loyalty and labor, was to be named director of the new Richard Nixon Center for Peace and Freedom in Washington; and Strobe Talbott, a presidential insider who became Clinton's Deputy Secretary of State in February 1994, amidst speculation that he would soon replace Warren Christopher as the nation's chief diplomat. Talbott worked closely with James Collins at the State Department and Nicholas Burns of the National Security Council staff at the White House. Talbott, Collins, and Burns, all well informed and articulate, shared Clinton's admiration for the former president and enjoyed the process of conferring with him. "Nixon," one official told me, "reads everything. He's truly remarkable. His wisdom and experience are unmatched."

Although President Clinton was absorbed primarily with such domestic issues as health care, crime, and jobs, he understood that he was responsible for directing the foreign policy of the one superpower to have survived the Cold War. In his dealings with Moscow, he realized that he was sailing in uncharted and dangerous waters, and he sought guidance from many sources outside his administration, including senior senators, scholars, journalists, and Western entrepreneurs with personal experience doing business in Russia. He needed Republican support on Capitol Hill to finance his policy of helping Russia advance toward his dream of democracy and a free market economy. Nixon shared the dream and could provide the support. At the same time, there was always the possibility that Nixon might go on the offensive if he did not approve of Clinton's policy. Until the day he died, Nixon remained a hovering presence that Clinton felt he could ignore only at his political peril, and as such Nixon exercised a degree of influence over the president's Russia policy out of all proportion to his real status and position.

* * *

So commandingly did Nixon's views on Russia come to dominate official Washington that serious alternatives were rarely considered at the White House or the State Department. One Clinton aide, visiting the Kennedy School in 1993, when asked to explain the president's "let's roll up our sleeves and help Russia" policy, found herself saying: "If democracy fails in Russia, then there will be a new Cold War. There will be terrible challenges to our national security. We used to spend many billions on the Cold War. What Clinton is asking for is minimal stuff, chicken feed really, not much when you consider what we once spent defending ourselves against the Russians."

When a member of the faculty pointed out that she was using a policy formulation that could have been lifted from one of Nixon's op-ed pieces in the *Times*, she shuddered. She had accurately echoed the White House line, but the White House line was indistinguishable from the Nixon line. As one of the few at the White House for whom Watergate was still a living memory, she had objected to the Clinton-Nixon meeting, and she later conceded that she had uncritically accepted a policy laden with real and potential pitfalls that deserved deeper study.

On several occasions, starting with his "great" meeting with Nixon on March 9, 1993, Clinton publicly embraced the former president's approach to Russia. "We have been pretty much on the same wavelength on this issue. . . . He gave me a lot of very good ideas." In fact, Nixon's three central ideas became the questionable cornerstones of the president's policy.

First, Yeltsin was the indispensable leader, a committed democrat and the kingpin of Russian reform, and his faction, above all others in Moscow's fractious politics, had to be supported by the United States and other members of the G-7. Nixon rang a thousand alarm bells warning that if Yeltsin were toppled from power, "democracy" in Russia would wither and die. An embittered Mikhail Gorbachev objected to this assessment. "You think it's either Yeltsin or the bad guys," he told reporter Lee Hockstader (*Washington Post*, October 13, 1993, p. B1). "Very profound analysis. Amazingly profound analysis." Gorbachev's sarcasm was obvious. "People in the West tend to support Yeltsin just because he is for private property. . . . Does that mean he is a democrat? Why is the West making these incantations . . . supporting Yeltsin, Yeltsin,

Yeltsin? They're making Yeltsin believe that he has been acting correctly these past two years . . . when in fact we are on the verge of disintegration."

It was not just Gorbachev who raised questions about Washington's exclusive reliance on Yeltsin. No less a figure than Sergei Stankevich, an early Yeltsin ally and one of the new parliament's more impressive personalities, concluded that the Clinton administration had good working relations with fewer Russian politicians than even the Bush administration, and that this was a major blunder. Stankevich argued that Yeltsin was an increasingly vulnerable leader, who might collapse under the weight of his accumulating troubles and responsibilities and leave the United States in the awkward position of having to establish a working relationship with a new, relatively unknown successor harboring suspicions about America's former love affair with Yeltsin (*Washington Post*, August 10, 1993, p. A15).

Nixon's second contribution to administration policy was his insistence that Russia not only had the need for large-scale Western aid but also had the capacity to absorb it and use it to develop a democratic system. It took Nixon until March 1994 to revise his view. Robert Blackwill, a co-author with Graham Allison of the 1991 "grand bargain" linking Russia and America in "immediate, comprehensive and potent cooperation," changed his mind months earlier. Writing in the *Washington Post* on October 12, 1993, Blackwill acknowledged that "objective conditions are no longer ripe for such an ambitious undertaking, if they ever were" (p. A19).

Clinton had succeeded in enlisting bipartisan congressional support (thanks, in part, to Nixon) and in focusing G-7 attention on the challenge of drumming up aid for Russia. Unfortunately, he accepted Nixon's assumption that Russia had the infrastructure necessary to absorb and channel the aid into essential projects.

Russia had and has no such infrastructure—and Clinton and Nixon should have known better and rooted their policy in more realistic soil. Both Clinton and Nixon were woefully late in appreciating the way in which waste, inefficiency, and corruption, so commonly associated with the old Soviet *nomenklatura* were impeding progress. Enormous roadblocks were created, blatant obstructions to sensible, orderly reform. It was estimated that 30 percent to 50 percent of the foreign aid sent to Russia was diverted into middlemen's pockets or Swiss bank accounts.

Clinton and Nixon should also have resisted the temptation to put a Western clock on Russia's pace of economic reform. In urging the passage of a Western aid package by Congress, Clinton aides were wildly unrealistic about Russia's capacity to stick to a schedule recommended by foreign advisers. They failed to consider such issues as a meaningful safety net for Russian workers who would be dislocated in the predictable upheaval created by the effort to build a market economy. As *New York Times* columnist A. M. Rosenthal stressed on October 5, 1993, while "a country's freedom is our business, the exact pace of its move towards complete removal of price controls or job guarantees is not" (p. A27).

In addition, the international financial institutions through which Western aid was funneled continued to impose such stringent conditions that, as of mid-1993, less than half of the promised aid had actually been delivered. What followed was an unfortunate backlash. A sizable number of Russians who were initially enthusiastic about Western aid became frustrated by the delays and reluctantly concluded that the United States never had any real intention of delivering a major aid package and that it was concealing a sinister plot to keep Russia forever locked in a subservient position.

The final Nixon contribution was the notion, born of hubris

and historical miscalculation, that the West—the United States, in particular—held the key to Russia's future. Of course, President Clinton and his Secretary of State paid lip service to the idea that only Russia could determine its own future, but their actions suggested a different view—that the United States had won the Cold War and, as the world's surviving superpower, had the right to impose its own democratic values on the less fortunate nations of the world, including Russia, Ukraine, Belarus, and other republics of the former Soviet Union. They seemed to have persuaded themselves that such a task had become America's new manifest destiny. As columnist Stephen S. Rosenfeld wrote in the *Washington Post* on April 2, 1993, it was the very height of "ideological vanity" for the United States to assume that it could "lock Russia" into a future founded upon such exotic Western imports as "democracy and the free market."

A "senior Western diplomat" in Moscow summed up the problem in a conversation with *New York Times* correspondent Steven Erlanger (August 29, 1993). "In some very predictable ways," he explained, "the American effort to help Yeltsin has backfired. Of course the conservatives have distorted it. But foreigners cannot tell Russians what their national interests are." It was not surprising that right-wing newspapers such as *Trud* and *Red Star* were publishing blisteringly anti-American editorials attacking Washington's "outrageously cynical" and "unceremonious interference in the domestic affairs of Russia and a number of abutting states." But even *Moscow News,* one of Russia's most liberal newspapers, blasted the "purely American arrogance of power."

The administration's attitude was reflected in Presidential Decision Directive 13, a White House plan in the fall of 1993 to incorporate U.S. military power into a significant U.N. peacekeeping force to help resolve ethnic disputes in the former Soviet Union.

Although, between plan and implementation, there were many opportunities for reconsideration, news of Directive 13 sent shock waves through the Russian foreign and defense ministries and provided newly emerging ultranationalists in Moscow with "proof" that the West intended to "occupy" their country.

Despite these indications of trouble, Clinton, encouraged by Christopher, Talbott, and Nixon, pursued an essentially optimistic policy based on the assumption that Russia was transforming itself into a less developed version of the United States. It might be a bumpy ride, but after a period of shock therapy the economy would improve and democracy, or a close approximation of it, would follow. This romantic reverie was shattered by two bursts of Russian reality in October and December 1993. By year's end, Clinton's policy lay in shambles.

First, Yeltsin and the Russian parliament, constantly at odds over the political and economic future of the country, galloped toward an irreconcilable crisis. Not for the first time, Yeltsin denounced his opponents and threatened to disband the parliament, chosen under the old Communist system, and replace it with a popularly elected parliament, which would presumably support his reformist policies. This time, he acted. He closed parliament. His opponents, led by parliamentary leader Ruslan Khasbulatov and Vice-President Alexander Rutskoi, a retired general and war hero, reacted by seizing control of the "White House," which had been the symbol of Russian democracy during the 1991 coup attempt. They issued a string of defiant proclamations, leading on October 3–4 to armed rebellion against the state. Moscow echoed to rifle and machine gun fire and the rumbling of tanks. Rutskoi dispatched troops to Ostankino to take control of Moscow television. Yeltsin stalled for what seemed like an eternity before ordering Red Army troops and tanks to crush the rebellion. From a hundred yards away, troops fired shells into the "White House."

One-hundred forty-seven Russians were killed, hundreds of others wounded. Rutskoi and Khasbulatov were seized and imprisoned. The revolution that had been largely bloodless up to that point had finally turned violent.

Clinton supported Yeltsin's suppression of the rebellion and sent Secretary of State Christopher to Moscow to confer with the Russian leader. Nixon backed the administration's position. In for a penny, Clinton went in for a pound, believing that he had no realistic option other than to support Yeltsin. He announced that Vice-President Al Gore would visit Russia after the new parliamentary elections set for December 12, 1993, and that he himself would visit Moscow on January 13–15, 1994. U.S. diplomats in Moscow, anxious not to offend Yeltsin, cut their limited contacts with other pro-reform Russian politicians, who were developing serious second thoughts about Yeltsin's appetite for power at a time when it seemed as if his grip on power was weakening.

The December 1993 elections were seen by the White House as an opportunity to strengthen Yeltsin and advance the democratic process in Russia. But Russia pulled another surprise. The elections were democratic, but the results stunned democrats in Moscow and Washington. The ultranationalistic Liberal Democratic Party headed by Vladimir Zhirinovsky, whom Nixon would later label a "holy fool" (*New York Times,* March 25, 1994, p. A29), zoomed out of the electoral void to capture 24 percent of the popular vote. The Russian Communist Party, until recently so totally discredited, placed second in a field of splintered parties. The reformers—loosely associated with Yeltsin, who swung from frenzied activism in October to a puzzling, Gaullist aloofness during the campaign—were humiliated.

Pollsters concluded that it was not so much that the Russian people had voted for Zhirinovsky, a relative unknown until he launched a final television blitz with foreign money and expertise, but, rather, that they had voted against Yeltsin. Disillusioned by reforms that had been oversold, frightened by an erratic economy and streets suddenly controlled by Mafia criminals, they voted for the glib sloganeering of extremists and nationalists, who promised security at home, a return to empire, and ample food at afford-able prices.

It was into this Moscow blizzard of uncertainty and change that President Clinton flew on January 13, 1994. Before his departure, he conferred with his senior advisers and, on the phone, with Nixon. Should he continue to embrace Yeltsin? In a sense, the question answered itself. If Clinton proceeded with his plans for a Moscow visit, he had to embrace Yeltsin, who remained the country's president and outstanding proponent of reform. Other-wise the trip had no point. Since no one recommended that Clin-ton cancel his Moscow trip, he decided that again he had no real alternative: he would support reform and Yeltsin—in that order.

During the summit, Clinton and Yeltsin ("Bill" and "Boris" in their private negotiations) discussed Russia's future. Bill pledged Western aid for Russian reform, and Boris pledged continued dedication to a program of reform. Both presidents seemed to be stuck in the nostalgia and rhetoric of the past while the reality of Russia rushed past them. Within a week after Clinton left Mos-cow, Yeltsin's two closest pro-reform economic advisers abruptly quit. Yegor Gaidar and Boris Fedorov explained that Yeltsin had abandoned their program. Victor Chernomyrdin, the centrist prime minister, who once said he considered reform to be "ro-mantic," suddenly moved into a commanding political position in the Kremlin hierarchy. Zhirinovsky became a major figure in the newly convened Russian parliament, or Duma, his supporters placed in prominent positions with their power still to be tested. Foreign Minister Andrei Kozyrev, responding to the obvious drift to the right, began to push a tougher, more nationalistic line in foreign policy. In 1992, during a post-Soviet honeymoon period when U.S. and Russian diplomats gloried in talk of a "strategic partnership," he had spoken about "universal values" and denounced "force" as an instrument of national policy. Now he resurrected Brezhnev-era language and attacked the "military industrial complex" and "reactionary forces" in the United States and argued that Russia must defend its national interests, using "force," if necessary. Russian diplomats suddenly popped up in Bosnia and on CNN, and they again reminded Washington of their interests in the Middle East.

Nixon, even at age eighty-one, was too restless to observe these developments from the pastoral quiet of his home and office at Woodcliff Lake, New Jersey. He wanted to return to Moscow and see for himself. He instructed Simes to arrange yet another visit—his tenth since 1959 and his fifth since 1986—and to tell President Clinton of his plans. Like any other reader of the *New York Times* and watcher of MacNeil-Lehrer, Nixon could see the deterioration in U.S.–Russian relations, but he wanted to know more—and do more. His image as an elder statesman and his value to the Clinton administration rested on continually updated insights and impressions that he could get only from a visit to Moscow, the sort of visit he had made in 1992 and again in 1993.

Simes, using all of his contacts in Washington and Moscow, set about organizing a crowded ten-day visit in March, which was to include meetings with Yeltsin, other top government officials, and leaders of the conservative political opposition, including Zhirinovsky and Gennady Zyuganov, head of the Russian Communist Party. Simes also tried to arrange a meeting with Rutskoi, who, by a parliamentary decree of February 26, 1994, had been released from prison over Yeltsin's strenuous objection. Formally, Nixon's invitation came from Vladimir Lukin, a former ambassador to Washington and now chairman of the Foreign Affairs Committee of Russia's Duma.

On the U.S. side, Simes consulted with administration officials, such as Talbott, Lake, and Burns. They stressed, when questioned by reporters, that Nixon's trip was strictly private and unofficial, but they approved his itinerary, checked his list of scheduled meetings, and coordinated with the U.S. Embassy in Moscow and the Russian Foreign Ministry. Burns even traveled to Woodcliff Lake to brief Nixon on the latest U.S. intelligence about recent developments in Moscow, and a few days before Nixon's actual departure, on March 3, 1994, Clinton again called him and, according to Simes, explicitly approved of his plans to meet with Rutskoi and Zhirinovsky. Officials described Nixon's trip as "a fact-finding mission" (*Washington Post,* March 10, 1994, p. A33).

Nixon arrived in Moscow on Sunday, March 6, and left on March 16, 1994, for a one-day stopover in Kiev, capital of Ukraine, before flying on to London and Bonn. Though he expected the kind of cordial high-level treatment he had received on his two preceding trips, he was to be disappointed, primarily because, in two ways, Simes unintentionally offended Yeltsin.

First, in an op-ed article in the *New York Times* headlined "Is Yeltsin Losing His Grip?" published on the day Nixon arrived in Moscow, Simes wrote that "it is an open secret that he is not in full control of his country—or even his own cabinet." Simes argued that it was time for the United States to look beyond Yeltsin, and he mentioned as "acceptable alternatives" the names of Grigory Yavlinsky, the economist who had advocated the "grand bargain" of 1991; Sergei Shakhrai, a moderate reformer who was Minister of Nationalities; and Prime Minister Chernomyrdin himself (*New York Times,* March 6, 1994, section 4, p. 15). Given Simes's closeness to Nixon and the Clinton administration, the

Russian Embassy in Washington must have faxed a copy of the op-ed piece to the Foreign Ministry in Moscow for Yeltsin's perusal.

Second, on Monday, his first full day in Moscow, Nixon began his scheduled meetings with Russia's leaders by traveling to the home of Rutskoi, who had masterminded the violent uprising against Yeltsin in October. This proved to be a snafu of major proportions. For in Yeltsin's rogues' gallery of political enemies, the former vice-president occupied the number-one spot. Final arrangements for this Nixon-Rutskoi meeting had been completed only the day before, and though Simes informed U.S. Ambassador Thomas Pickering and a few key Russian officials that the meeting was to take place, he should have been sensitive enough to anticipate Yeltsin's fury.

Reporters and cameramen recorded the scene—Nixon in his customary dark suit and Rutskoi in a casual argyle sweater, both smiling and shaking hands in front of a colorful, caged parrot. On Russian television that evening, this cheerful scene of Nixon and Rutskoi appeared as a lead item on the news. In a Russian context Nixon seemed to be honoring Rutskoi. Here was a prominent foreigner engaged in a warm, friendly chat with the man who had only recently led an armed insurrection against Yeltsin and the Russian state. Nixon, no stranger to quests for political rehabilitation, should have known that by seeing Rutskoi when he did and how he did, he was helping the former vice-president with his own rehabilitation. The world service of the ITAR-TASS news agency in Moscow put a Russian spin on Nixon's decision to see Rutskoi. "Nixon did not take into account peculiarities of the current political situation and the political mentality of Russians" (BBC Summary of World Broadcasts, March 15, 1994, part 1, SU/ 1946/B). Translation: Yeltsin and Rutskoi hated each other.

The following day, March 8, 1994, Nixon met with Zyuganov,

head of the Russian Communist Party. The meeting was scheduled to last twenty minutes; it went on for an hour and a half. Nixon emerged to tell reporters that Yeltsin's political opponents seemed to reject the use of force and a return to the old days.

Zyuganov told me that he had been extremely impressed by Nixon's grasp of Russian affairs (interview, April 4, 1994). "It is a matter of no importance to me that President Nixon once led an anti-Communist crusade. He understands our problems now, and he wants to help. He is very smart. He has connections. I respect him." I asked Zyuganov to compare Nixon's understanding of global politics to Clinton's. A smile creased his round, Slavic face, the kind of face one used to see on gigantic posters on Communist holidays. During a visit to the United States, Zyuganov did not want to make waves. "I shall not answer that question," he said.

On Wednesday, March 9, 1994, while Yeltsin was participating in a Kremlin ceremony honoring the late Yuri Gagarin, who in 1961 became the first man in space, the burly leader turned to reporters and cameras and, in comments that seemed both angry and impromptu, he canceled all government meetings with Nixon, including his own, which was set for the following Monday. "The former American president met with Rutskoi and Zyuganov," said Yeltsin, chopping the air with his right hand, "and he was coming here to meet with me. How can one come to a country and look for the dark spots? Let him know that Russia is a great country—and to play with it in this way, I want one thing today and tomorrow another, that won't work now. No. After this, I will not meet him. And the government will not meet him" (*New York Times*, March 10, 1994, p. A5). That evening, Yeltsin's decision to snub Nixon led the newscasts on Moscow television, and it dominated political discussions in newsrooms and embassies.

Nixon and Simes were stunned. They soon learned that they

no longer had access to government transportation or security. One after another, appointments were being canceled. Should Nixon pack up and leave? The question was considered and rejected. There was still much to do and many Russians to see. By the time the resourceful Simes held a news conference a few hours later, he had already conferred with Ambassador Pickering and with key Russian officials. Even the White House was alerted to Yeltsin's decision. In this age of instant communications, the president of the United States was immediately involved in the dispute, and he leaped to Nixon's defense. It's "not the end of the world," Clinton said, but "I wish [Yeltsin] would see him, because I think they would enjoy talking to one another" (*Washington Post,* March 10, 1994, p. A33). Clinton had no problem with Nixon's seeing Rutskoi. Referring to his farewell phone call with Nixon, the president added, "I said he should meet with whomever he wanted and I'd be interested to hear his reports when he got back" (*New York Times,* March 10, 1994, p. A5). "President Yeltsin should not assume that Mr. Nixon is not friendly toward his administration and toward democracy and toward reform, because, quite the contrary, he's been a very strong supporter of our policy for the last year. And I wouldn't overreact to the fact that he met with some people who are in opposition to the president" (*Atlanta Constitution,* March 9, 1994, section A, p. 1). Clinton seemed to be missing a key point. It was not that Yeltsin objected to Nixon's seeing "some people . . . in the opposition"; it was that Yeltsin objected to Nixon's seeing Rutskoi.

In Moscow, Simes seemed to be missing the same point. Perhaps, to cover his own embarrassment, he missed the point deliberately. "I am surprised, first of all," he said, obviously speaking for Nixon, "that President Yeltsin would not find anybody but an 81-year-old former U.S. President, who is his friend and Russia's friend, to reassert his macho and to tell us that Russia is a great country." On Nixon's reaction: "He is puzzled. He is disappointed. But . . . he is a big boy, and he has had his share of disappointments in his life, some of them much more serious than this one. He will manage" (*New York Times*, March 10, 1994, p. A5). Later, Simes added, "There is something smallminded about this situation. For someone who is described by our Secretary of State as the best hope for Russian democracy, this kind of intolerance of dissent . . . raises a lot of questions" (*Boston Globe*, March 10, 1994, p. 2).

The Yeltsin/Nixon flap became big news. The *Washington Post* bought the Simes-Nixon line and ran an editorial, "Not Your Ordinary Tourist," which praised Nixon's "unexceptionable" conduct and questioned Yeltsin's continued capacity to govern. "People," wrote the *Post* editors, "are beginning to look beyond him and his time" (*Washington Post*, March 11, 1994, p. A24). Kozyrev, surely not one of those "people," placed the blame squarely on Simes. Describing the Nixon trip as "ill thought out," the foreign minister compared Nixon's meeting with Rutskoi as "roughly equivalent" to going to a "respectable gathering" and using the "toilet" with the doors open and then rejoining the "guests" (BBC, March 15, 1994, SU/1944 B/5; "Itogi" program on Russian TV, March 10, 1994).

Nixon tried to take the high ground, knowing that behind the scenes U.S. and Russian diplomats were frantically trying to contain the damage. At a reception hosted by Ambassador Pickering, Nixon praised both Clinton and Yeltsin as "partners, not just in peace, but partners in freedom throughout the world. . . . Democratic Russia, under the courageous leadership of Boris Yeltsin, gave the knockout blow to Soviet Communism" (*Washington Post*, March 11, 1994, p. A19). "I came here as his friend and I remain his friend. I wish him well" (*Boston Globe*, March 11, 1994, p. 2). Nixon's words, deliberately chosen to convey the impression of a diplomatic apology, were aimed at Yeltsin, and the Russian leader heard each one of them. By Saturday, March 12, 1994, Yeltsin had lifted his ban on government officials' meeting with Nixon, easing the strain on U.S.–Russian relations, but he left for a two-week vacation at the Black Sea resort of Sochi, explaining that his mother-in-law had died and therefore he could not arrange a convenient time to meet with Nixon (*Chicago Tribune,* March 14, 1994, p. 7). It was Yeltsin's way of saving face while burying the hatchet.

Lukin concluded that the controversy had been blown out of proportion. "Typichesky Amerikansky happy ending," he said (*Newsday,* March 15, 1994, p. 15).

* * *

Controversy, by definition, generates news coverage, and Levitas and Nixon arranged for another op-ed submission to the *New York Times* before the former president had even returned from Moscow. According to a National Security Council official, Nixon's *Times* piece, which appeared on March 25, 1994, was closely patterned after his private report to Clinton. It carried the headline "Moscow, March '94: Chaos and Hope," and it marked a distinct change in tone and content for Nixon.

No longer was the former president brimming with optimism that a pro-Western democracy and a market economy were taking hold in Russia. Indeed, he wrote: "The Russia I saw on this trip is a very different nation from the one I visited just one year ago. . . . A strongly pro-American attitude has in many cases become disturbingly anti-American" (*New York Times,* March 25, 1994, p. A29).

Though Nixon complimented Yeltsin in Moscow, in his op-ed piece he criticized "his frequent absences from Moscow" and "his increasingly erratic conduct," adding that "over the centuries, rev-

olutionary leaders have not been good nation builders." Yeltsin
has lost "much of the mystique from his historic role in the de-
struction of Soviet Communism," but the United States should
still "treat him with respect." He is "the first freely elected President in Russian history," and he is still "the country's most popular politician."

If, in Nixon's judgment, Yeltsin was losing his touch, then the
United States should begin to "pay more attention to the new
generation of Russian leaders"—"many of whom I met"—and
he listed the same handful of relatively young politicians Simes
had cited in his *Times* piece of March 6, 1994: Yavlinsky, Shakhrai,
and, of course, Chernomyrdin, "the front-runner to succeed Yeltsin." Nixon even spoke in relatively favorable terms about Yeltsin's political opponents—"and I met with them all"—Zyuganov,
Zhirinovsky, and Rutskoi. He seemed to feel the need to stress
that he had met them all as a way of adding authenticity to his
judgments. They had "assured" Nixon that they would pursue
their objectives "through constitutional means." Zyuganov, "an
impressive Communist Party hardliner," was quoted as saying that
Russia could never return to Communism. "We cannot cross the
same river twice." Zhirinovsky, though "a ruthless, shrewd dema-
gogue," "will not be elected President of Russia." "He lacks the
presence and conviction to lead a great nation."

Nixon expressed serious concern about Russia's domestic
scene ("chaotic") and about Russia's foreign policy, which, he said,
had experienced "a sea change" since the December elections.
Just as he had bluntly warned the Foreign Affairs Committee of
the Russian Duma that there were "some profoundly disturbing
developments" recently in U.S.-Russian relations (*Boston Globe,*
March 15, 1994, p. 26), so he warned the readers of the *Times*, "We
are great world powers, and our interests will inevitably clash, but
the greatest mistake we can make is to try to drown differences in

champagne and vodka toasts at 'feel-good' summit meetings.'"
Was he indirectly criticizing Clinton's Bill-Boris summit of January? "The highest art of diplomacy is not to paper over irresoluble
differences with gobbledygook, but to find a way to disagree without damaging profoundly important strategic relationships." Specifically, he said, Russia could not be given a veto over "a NATO
decision to expand." Poland, Hungary, and the Czech Republic
had applied for admission, but the United States, sensitive to Russia's strategic concerns, had proposed a compromise formula,
called Partnership for Peace, which amounted to a form of loose
association with NATO but not full membership in NATO.

In this generally gloomy assessment of the U.S.-Russian relationship, nothing seemed to worry Nixon more than the "independence of Ukraine," which he described as "indispensable." If
Russia and Ukraine were to come to blows, Bosnia would "look
like a Sunday-school picnic." In what appeared to be a warning
directed at the White House, Nixon asserted: "Moscow should be
made to understand that any attempt to destabilize Ukraine—to
say nothing of outright aggression—would have devastating consequences for the Russian-American relationship. Ukrainian stability is in the strategic interest of the United States." Again Nixon
was using powerful words, but his meaning was not clear. Was he
recommending that the United States break relations with Russia,
or go to war against Russia, if Russia threatened or actually
attacked Ukraine?

Finally, in a major overhaul of his own policy recommendations, Nixon blasted the U.S. aid program for Russia. "Rip-offs,
shakedowns and outright corruption among recipients, along
with incompetence among administrators, have combined to create enormous disillusionment." He then advised President Clinton "to order an immediate, comprehensive review of aid to Russia and the other former Soviet states before Congress forces him

to do so." Speaking to his own GOP supporters and admirers on Capitol Hill, Nixon concluded: "Mr. Clinton deserves bipartisan support on providing adequate aid to the forces of freedom in Russia. But this support should be hardheaded, without illusions about Russian conduct and without sacrifice of U.S. interests."

Again, what did Nixon mean by "adequate" support? Who were the "forces of freedom"? And, given the "rip-offs, shake-downs and outright corruption," about which he had just warned, how could any aid be sent to Russia?

Clearly, there had been a significant shift in Nixon's approach to aiding Russia. No longer was he pushing for an "urgent" and "massive" aid package. No longer was he recommending tens of billions of dollars of Western aid or projecting even more in private investment. And no longer was he even referring to his already-scaled-back version of "targeted" aid. Now Nixon was appealing directly to the president to review the entire aid program before Congress forced his hand by simply shutting it down completely. The fact is, from the very beginning, Nixon had never seriously thought through the many complexities involved in launching and sustaining a comprehensive aid program to Russia. He simply used it as a rallying cry, assuming wrongly that money could buy a major part of the solution in revolutionary Russia.

Two days after the *Times* published Nixon's bleak report, the *Post* published Simes's even bleaker report (*Washington Post*, March 27, 1994, p. C1). "The Yeltsin era is coming to an end," Simes began. "In Moscow today, one hears all sorts of rumors—of an impending palace coup or a life-threatening disease. . . . The Russian president today is a lonely man without a well-defined program. . . . Moscow today is reminiscent of the last days of the Brezhnev regime. . . . Nobody expects the regime to last and, accordingly, treats the leader as a lame duck." Simes painted Yeltsin as a pitiful figure who went "ballistic" after the Nixon/Rutskoi meeting. Simes quoted one of Yeltsin's associates: "Seeing this criminal on TV standing next to Nixon was offensive to him." The fault, according to Simes, rested squarely on Yeltsin's growing isolation and insecurity. But then shouldn't a Russian expert of Simes's reputation have anticipated the problem—and therefore avoided it?

* * *

In March 1994 a White House official described U.S. policy toward Russia as a "crap shoot." "You put your money on a hunch," he said, after a meeting with Nixon, "and then you hope that your man comes in. We are making a bet on the future." Like Nixon, he was highly pessimistic about Ukraine. "It could unravel as a nation within the next two or three years," he said. And then what? "I simply don't know. Strobe [Talbott] doesn't know. Nixon doesn't know. We'll have to do something, but we don't know what."

The only concrete step the administration took was to begin to reorganize its aid program to Russia and the former Soviet republics, perhaps in response to Nixon's recommendation that the program be reviewed. Instead of splitting the aid 65 percent for Russia and the remaining 35 percent for the other republics, as was the case up until the December elections, a decision was made to flip the priorities: over the next two years, 35 percent would go to Russia and 65 percent to the other republics, with Ukraine alone getting $700 million, putting it behind Egypt, Israel, and Russia as the fourth largest recipient of American foreign aid.

* * *

The Nixon-Clinton relationship was cut short by Nixon's death in April 1994, but there is no certainty about how long this odd partnership would have continued. It seems likely, judging from the excerpts from Nixon's last book published posthumously in *Time,* that Nixon had become tired of his role as a bipartisan elder statesman and was more comfortable reverting to his traditional role as a partisan Republican lambasting an incumbent Democratic president. Early in 1993, in a message conveyed to the administration by Roger Stone, Nixon had promised a year-long "moratorium" on criticism of the president's foreign policy in exchange for a White House meeting with Clinton. The moratorium had apparently run out. There was no resemblance between the "love letter" Nixon sent to Clinton in his op-ed piece of March 5, 1993, and his contemptuous dismissal of Clinton's policies in *Beyond Peace.*

Nixon's criticism of Clinton's domestic policies simply echoed the Republican line on Capitol Hill. He ripped into Clinton's health care plan, "all 1,342 impenetrable pages of it," as a "blueprint for the takeover by the Federal Government of one-seventh of the nation's economy. If enacted, it would represent the ultimate revenge of the 1960s generation." As for the massive budget deficit that Clinton was struggling to contain, Nixon dismissed the "liberal lament" that it had been caused by Reagan's cutting taxes and increasing the defense budget and blamed the "lingering legacies of the Great Society," a reference to Johnson's social programs of the 1960s.

But his sharpest barbs were reserved for Clinton's foreign policy. He dismissed the concept of "assertive multilateralism"—first advanced by the U.S. ambassador to the United Nations, Madeleine Albright, as a way of explaining the Clinton administration's reliance on U.N. cooperation in the post–Cold War world—as "naive diplomatic gobbledygook." He described the "debacle in Somalia" as "a lesson in how not to conduct U.S. foreign policy." He ridiculed the administration's vision of "free-market democracy," dubbed "enlargement" by some White House officials.

"'Enlargement' is a tricky word," Nixon wrote. "In photography, a negative can be enlarged to a three-by-five snapshot or a wall-size mural. Based on the record so far, the present Administration is aiming for a wallet-size." He referred to the "carnage in the former Yugoslavia" as "one of America's most unfortunate and unnecessary foreign policy failures." Regarding China, where he had a sort of proprietary interest, he lambasted Clinton's policy, accusing the president of responding to Chinese overtures "by increasing distrust, stirring up trouble, threatening non-cooperation and fomenting confrontation."

It was only when he turned to Russia that he refrained from condemning Clinton's policy; that would have been difficult, given the fact that Clinton had followed his advice. Nixon essentially took the line he had taken after his last trip to Moscow. For once he was uncertain about the correct course to follow, and he fell back on platitudes. He did not specifically raise the question of "Who lost Russia?" with all its political undercurrents, but he came close. He stressed that "no other single factor will have a greater political impact on the world" in the twenty-first century than "whether political and economic freedom take root and thrive in Russia and the other former communist nations." He drew a direct line from Moscow to the White House. "Today's generation of American leaders," he wrote, obviously meaning Clinton but not mentioning him by name, "will be judged primarily by whether they did everything possible to bring about this outcome. If they fail, the cost that their successors will have to pay will be unimaginably high."

In Nixon's view, Yeltsin was a key but no longer *the* key to building Russia's democracy. Yeltsin, he wrote, "is a tough and sometimes ruthless Russian patriot" who "should be supported but not idolized. By idealizing Yeltsin's government, the West runs the risk of personalizing its Russian policy and creating a potential trap for itself." Nixon conveniently seemed to forget that for the previous two years he had been Yeltsin's most ardent supporter and that he had urged Clinton to embrace the Russian leader. "If we do not develop good working relationships with the new generation of Russian leaders, we will be caught flat-footed by unexpected shifts in the political landscape."

Nixon then warned the Clinton administration about two potential "mistakes": the "most dangerous" would be to "drown" U.S.-Russian "differences" in "champagne and vodka toasts at feel-good summits"; and the second would be "to neglect our responsibility for assisting Russia in its transition to freedom, or arrogantly to scold or punish it for every foreign or domestic policy transgression, as though it were an international problem child." Here again was an inconsistency: in his last op-ed piece in the *Times*, Nixon had urged Clinton to "review" all American aid programs to Russia in light of recent political developments.

* * *

Though his initial policy recommendations had failed, Nixon had succeeded. Taking advantage of an unusual combination of circumstances—the dramatic developments in Russia that began in 1991; the chaos and confusion of the post–Cold War world; the shift from a Republican "foreign policy" president unwilling to adopt a bold plan for Russia to a Democratic "domestic policy" president insecure about his national security credentials and eager to win conservative support—Nixon established a position for himself as a wise, seasoned adviser with top-level contacts in Washington and Moscow. His writings, his travel, and his access to the White House even with a Democratic president gave him the perfect opportunity to shape the writing of his own history.

CHAPTER

12

THE FINAL NIXON

On Monday, April 18, 1994, Nixon, at home in New Jersey, received page proofs of *Beyond Peace,* which was scheduled for publication in June. Random House was hoping to advance the publication date for competitive reasons: H. R. Haldeman's *Diaries,* reportedly containing "new revelations" about Watergate, would appear in bookstores by mid-May. To satisfy Random House, Nixon had been busy updating the manuscript ever since his return from Moscow. Though tired, perhaps more than he even realized, he had also been considering a return trip to Moscow after getting a personal invitation from Yeltsin, who was obviously contrite about his abrupt decision to cancel a scheduled meeting with Nixon during his March visit.

Shortly before dinner, the thirty-seventh president of the United States suffered a massive stroke. He was rushed to a New York hospital. On Tuesday night his condition worsened. On Thursday he slipped into a deep coma. The Reverend Billy Graham, a family friend who was consoling Nixon's two daughters, Tricia and Julie, and their families, asked President Clinton to deliver one of the eulogies at the funeral service, which was already being planned by a few of Nixon's former advance men. It was to be at the Nixon Library in Yorba Linda, California, not in Washington, where memories of Watergate might mar the occasion. Clinton agreed. A White House aide later explained that the presi-

dent "had everything to gain and nothing to lose by acting mag-
nanimously and assuming a proper presidential dignity" (*New York
Times,* April 25, 1994, p. B8).

On Friday, April 22, 1994, at 9:08 P.M., Richard Nixon died, but
there was no immediate bulletin. The official announcement was
made by none other than the president of the United States, who
spoke from the Rose Garden shortly after 11:00 P.M. It was carried
"live" by all television networks.

Clinton spoke of his "sad duty" to inform the "people of the
United States" of Nixon's death. "I was deeply grateful," the
Democratic president said, "for his wise counsel on so many occasions on many issues over the last year. . . . He gave of himself
with intelligence and devotion to duty, and his country owes him
a debt of gratitude for that service."

He then talked more informally about his remarkably cooperative relationship with the late president. "We made contact with
each other shortly after—I think shortly after the election. Either
that or shortly after I came in here," Clinton said, ignoring on this
occasion the fact that he had stiffed Nixon's repeated overtures
for a meeting until early March 1993. "I had him up to the White
House for a visit. We talked frequently on the phone. I sought his
advice about a number of issues in foreign policy, and we talked
quite a lot about Russia." Then, referring specifically to Nixon's
March visit to Moscow, the president continued: "We had a good
long visit right before he went to Russia, and just a month ago
today, I think, he penned his last letter . . . of his thoughts on that
trip and his advice. So our relationship continued to be warm and
constructive throughout the period of my presidency, and he went
out of his way to give me his best advice. And I was incredibly
impressed with the energy and the vigor, and frankly the rigor
that he brought to analyzing this issue."

Gerald Ford, Jimmy Carter, Ronald Reagan, and George Bush,

who had also experienced the glory and burden of the American presidency, quickly followed Clinton's announcement with praise of their own, ushering in a remarkable ten-day period of positive comment about Nixon from journalists and politicians, Republicans and Democrats alike.

The following day, Clinton, determined, as David Gergen explained, "to do this in a first-rate way," extended full honors to Nixon. He ordered American flags to be flown at half-mast for thirty days, and he declared April 27, 1994, the day of Nixon's funeral, to be a "national day of mourning."

That evening, while Clinton was attending the annual dinner of the White House Correspondents Association, he felt the need to break into the usual frivolity with a few serious reflections about the late president. "The thing that impressed me about Nixon," Clinton said, "was that he had a tenacious refusal to give up on his own involvement in this country and the world. . . . I think we should all try to remember when we are tempted to write off anybody because of our differences with them that we share a common humanity."

Over the next few days, newspapers and television were filled with remembrances of Nixon. *Time, Newsweek,* and *U.S. News & World Report* ran long cover stories. Though there was competing news, including a historic election in South Africa and a bloody siege in Bosnia, coverage of Nixon dominated the airwaves, rising to a dignified crescendo at 7 P.M., EDT, on April 27, 1994, when the networks began an hour and a half of "live" coverage of the funeral that was beamed around the world.

Television elevated the event beyond simple sorrow. The dignified daughters, the solemn lineup of all four living ex-presidents—Ford, Carter, Reagan, and Bush—with their wives, next to President and Mrs. Clinton, the presence of so many senators and representatives, the faces from twenty years before, the reverential cadence of the television anchors: all spoke of a special moment in American politics, when an era associated with the stormy career of Richard Nixon came to an end. Not since 1973, when Lyndon Johnson died, had the nation experienced a presidential funeral. At that time President Nixon, besieged by the Watergate scandal, attended the funeral in the Capitol Rotunda but did not speak.

Under uncharacteristically gray California skies, a flag-covered casket rested on a wooden platform in front of Nixon's boyhood home, shaded by a huge oak tree. A U.S. Navy choir sang hymns and patriotic songs. Hundreds of invited guests and thousands of mourners heard four eulogies, delivered by former Secretary of State Kissinger, Senator Dole, California Governor Pete Wilson, and President Clinton. Kissinger, his gravelly voice trembling with emotion, described Nixon as "one of the seminal presidents" in foreign affairs. Dole said that the second half of the twentieth century would come to be known as "the age of Nixon," and then he wept. Wilson summed up Nixon's credo in life as "never, ever give up."

Clinton was undoubtedly aware—through the excerpts in *Time*—that in his last political comments Nixon had apparently decided to end his unusual honeymoon with a Democratic president. But he decided to take the high road in his own remarks about Nixon. He urged Americans to "remember President Nixon's life in totality." In a clear appeal for national and political reconciliation, Clinton said of the politician who had polarized the nation for decades, "May the day of judging President Nixon on anything less than his entire life and career come to a close." Clinton seemed to be saying that Nixon had to be judged on more than Watergate.

With this service, and its twenty-one-gun salute, indistinguishable from the honors paid to any other former president, it became clear that in a formal sense Nixon's twenty-year quest for renewed respectability had finally been crowned with success. His brother Edward, in an appearance on "Good Morning America," expressed the feeling of the family. "The response of the nation," he said, "seems finally to be coming around."

* * *

This rise to renewed respectability was no accident. It was the result of a carefully planned political campaign in which the press played a central role. Nixon's attitude toward the press, long before he reached the White House, was one of resentment, suspicion, and hostility. As president, in addition to placing illegal wiretaps on reporters' home phones, he used the powers of the government to harass and intimidate them in many other ways. After his resignation, his hostility toward the press took on a new and ironic dimension: since he had lost all his official power, he could no longer harass reporters; but since he still recognized their enormous capacity to influence public perceptions, he took to courting them with a persistent and highly sophisticated strategy of private lunches and dinners, meetings, memos, op-ed pieces, books, travel, interviews, and telephone conversations— and ultimately the strategy bore fruit. Many reporters found themselves captivated by this courtship, especially since the suitor carried the credentials of controversy and a surefire story. Other politicians have also tried to ingratiate themselves with the press, but many have found that this is a difficult pursuit with uncertain rewards, and not many have had Nixon's grit and doggedness, or his sense of what makes journalism tick.

Without the press as a major component of his overall strategy, all of Nixon's efforts on behalf of both Russia and his own rehabilitation would likely have failed. Imagine for a moment that he had written his memo but it had never leaked, that he had held his

Washington conference but his anti-Bush attack had not appeared on the front page of the *Times* the day before, that he had traveled to Moscow on several occasions but his calls for aid to Russia had never reached the op-ed page of the *Times*. What impact would Nixon have had on Bush and Clinton? On public opinion? On foreign policy? And, most important, on his own political rehabilitation? Minimal, if any. Nixon would still have been painted in the dark hues of Watergate, a smart, experienced, but amoral and vindictive politician.

Instead, during his final years, Nixon again became an actor on the diplomatic stage, an adviser to a president. He was widely seen as an "elder statesman" with a commendable mission. The newest Nixon seemed better in the winter of his life than he had been in the summer.

Few politicians have better understood the power of the press to affect public policy. When Nixon wanted to awaken Bush to the many challenges of the new Russia, he did not request a private meeting in the Oval Office. He did not ask for an urgent session with congressional leaders. He did not arrange another news conference on Capitol Hill. He did not organize a Sanhedrin of former presidents and Secretaries of State to issue a declaration of high principle. He turned to the press, the one institution in American public life capable of transforming his vision into policy. More specifically, he turned most often to the *New York Times* in recognition of its enormous influence in American journalism and politics. And because the *Times* was also television's most respected and valued tip sheet, he knew that he was, by way of a carom shot, directing his message at the tube as well.

Nixon was never casual about politics or the press. He watched, studied, analyzed, and discussed trends and changes with the dedication of a baseball fan checking the box scores every morning. After Watergate, with the arrival of a new generation of reform-minded politicians, party bosses and committee chairmen lost much of their former influence and a new form of political power came to be concentrated in the press. Many a savvy politician learned that he could advance his own agenda by establishing a good relationship with a handful of reporters and editors at certain key newspapers, magazines, and television networks.

Of course, this interaction between the politician and the press was not an alliance of compatible cultures. Quite the contrary. It was based on two contrasting cultures: the politician was intent on controlling the message, while the journalist was determined to spot the message, dissect it, and then report it in his own way. Tension between the two was natural and chronic. The press demanded the freedom, as guaranteed by the U.S. Constitution, to print and broadcast whatever it wished, and it did not want to be constrained by any legislative or institutional guidelines. It did not want to be lectured about its responsibilities to the community or the nation. It did not want to be part of the political process, though in fact it was; it wanted instead to play the role of a bulldog protecting the process.

Indeed, the very definition of news was now subject to broad disagreement: on the part of the press there was confusion about whether its role should be that of the fly on the wall of history or the agenda-setting agent of change in the community; and on the part of the politician there was often the tendency to see dark conspiracies in the normal chaotic functioning of a free press.

Take, for example, the publication of the Nixon memo by the *Post* and the *Times* on the day before the Nixon conference. To the uninformed citizen or official, its appearance in both papers was clear proof of journalistic conspiracy. How could there be anything innocent about the nation's two most prestigious newspapers running similar stories on the day before Nixon and Bush were to share the same platform and discuss the same subject of aid to Russia? According to this line of reasoning, the explanation had to be some kind of backdoor collusion. But that was not in fact the explanation; it was not collusion but coincidence.

In the case of the Nixon memo, the *Post* and the *Times* did not cooperate with each other, nor did they conspire on Nixon's behalf to damage the Bush administration. Indeed, their attitudes toward the memo and Nixon were quite different. The *Post* had Super Tuesday in mind, a well-rounded campaign story in which the Nixon memo was only one of a number of factors affecting Bush's prospects for reelection. The *Times* had the next day's Nixon conference in mind, a sharply focused story timed for maximum effect, in which Nixon attacked Bush on an issue of importance to both the Bush campaign and the nation. The *Post* produced a perfectly respectable story, well researched and written, but the *Times,* by focusing narrowly on Nixon's critique of Bush's policy and then plastering the story on the front page, attracted more attention and shaped the news flow on this issue not only for that day but for the rest of the year. What is news? There is no one commonly accepted definition.

For those who still see conspiracy in examples of overlapping reporting, there is a possible explanation in what is called "pack journalism," reporters who band together and cover the same story, the same sources, in the same way. Covering a campaign or the White House or any other story where a horde of journalists rush after a single institutional source can often yield the meager one-dimensional news product associated with "pack journalism." But, though a number of prominent news organizations may highlight similar stories, using virtually identical sources, this is not to be mistaken for conspiracy. It is only lazy journalism.

Among news people and organizations, there are now more and more forms of cooperation that are essentially the result of shrinking budgets and imaginations. For example, during the 1992 presidential campaign, many news organizations pooled their resources to cover the president, sending one camera team to shoot for all the networks on a routine trip. They shared exit poll data, and, continuing a practice they started several campaigns ago, newspapers and networks split the costs of polling prospective voters. CBS News and the *New York Times,* or NBC News and the *Wall Street Journal,* produced and used the same polling data, reinforcing what was right about their common analysis of the data and what was wrong with it. But on a story of the political and diplomatic magnitude of the Nixon memo, chance, judgment, and old-fashioned competition were still the paramount factors. They drove the game.

Starting with the memo, Nixon so smoothly seeded the political environment in Washington that his ideas came to be accepted as part of the conventional wisdom—what reporters told one another and then told their readers, viewers, or listeners, who spread the word to the pollsters and the politicians, who also watched and read and ultimately issued pronouncements and made decisions that reporters then communicated to the public—starting a new cycle, with its never-ending spin.

The interaction of press, politics, and public policy could be understood as a gigantic loop of information, not limited to Washington but global in scale, from which there is now no escape. Ideas, people, and politics are in constant motion, colliding at extraordinary speeds, like millions of tiny particles bumping into one another in a new technological universe, influencing and affecting almost everyone, sometimes deliberately but often without design or calculation and with surprising and unpredictable consequences.

In this modern loop, how could one measure Nixon's success in erasing the stain of Watergate? One approach might be a Lexis/Nexis search. Check the words "Nixon" combined with "Watergate" or "scandal" or "resignation," and what do the magical computer chips produce? Hardly a single story in the years before his death. For now Nixon has come to be associated not with the disgrace that drove him from office and embarrassed the nation but with Russia, aid, Bush, Clinton, U.S.-Russian relations, the future of the planet.

Another approach might be a review of press coverage of his funeral. The coverage was reverent on television and generally respectful in newspapers and magazines. The *Los Angeles Times* headlined its story, "Nixon Gets Hero's Farewell." *Time* described him as "the most important figure of the postwar era," and columnist Hugh Sidey wrote a warm goodbye. *Newsweek* concluded, "Death delivered to Richard Nixon what he coveted most over the last 20 years: reconciliation with the political establishment." The *Wall Street Journal* editorialized, "The final years may have been Richard Nixon's greatest triumph." Some assessments were more balanced, but so much of the copy was painted in the broad brushstrokes of revisionist flattery that Russell Baker of the *New York Times* cried out for a Mencken-like critique, Michael Gartner in *USA Today* blasted Nixon as the "corrupt leader of a corrupt administration," and Jonathan Yardley of the *Washington Post* concluded his column: "Day of Mourning, indeed! Good riddance is more like it."

Among the journalists writing the "first rough draft of history" about Nixon's final years there is clearly one school of thought that argues for tolerance. Nixon paid his dues, made his contribution—enough. If he sought a form of personal rehabilitation, if he wanted to help President Clinton formulate an effective policy toward Russia, and Clinton welcomed the help, then was this not a better use of presidential experience than spending one's time on a golf course or making speeches to Japanese corporations?

There is another school of thought that argues against a loss of historical memory or perspective. Especially in an age of contrived images, when the perception of reality is as acceptable as reality itself, all of Nixon must be remembered. In this sense, President Clinton was right to make the case for judging Nixon "in totality."

Nixon's chief claim to fame came in the area of foreign policy. He opened the door to China, but he had had a great deal to do with shutting the door in the late 1940s, when he raised the question of "Who lost China?" and paralyzed America's Asia policy for more than twenty years. His policy of détente with the Soviet Union reduced the chances of nuclear war, but it was less a new departure than the continuation of a process begun by his Democratic predecessors—Kennedy with the limited test ban treaty of 1963 and Johnson with the summit meeting at Glassboro in 1967—a process interrupted by the Soviet invasion of Czechoslovakia in 1968 and complicated by the growing American involvement in the Vietnam War. More than 30,000 Americans had already been killed in Vietnam when Nixon entered the presidency hinting at a secret plan to end the war. By the time it ended in April 1975, with no honor, no decent interval, only an ignominious American defeat, the only one in its proud history, another 27,557 Americans had been killed—for nothing; and this does not include the hundreds of thousands of Vietnamese, Laotians, and Cambodians who also died in the wake of the American involvement.

Nixon's one truly original contribution to world peace came in the Middle East, where in the course of the 1973 war he first saved Israel from possible defeat by opening an emergency pipeline of military supplies and then contrived to end the hostilities in such a way that the Arab states could claim they had not been defeated, thus opening the way to a peace process that continues to this day.

In domestic policy, Nixon continued a number of Great Society programs in a Republican guise, but he launched a "Southern strategy" in presidential politics that widened the gap between blacks and whites and reversed the civil rights progress of the 1960s.

Finally, there was Watergate. It happened only twenty years ago, and it poisoned the well of American politics. It ruptured the bond between the American people and their leaders that has begun to be restored only in recent years.

What, then, is the reporter's obligation to himself, to his family, to his craft, to his country? It is to tell the story.

MEMORIES OF WATERGATE

> I would simply point out that what distinguishes us as a group
> from those who came before and those who have come after
> is that we are too young to remember a time when Richard
> Nixon was not on the political scene and too old reasonably to
> expect that we shall live to see one.
>
> —Meg Greenfield, "My Generation Is Missing," *The Reporter*
> 36:35–36, May 4, 1967

Like many others of my generation, I grew up with Richard
Nixon.

In the late 1940s, when I was a teenager, Nixon was already
making news as a young politician from southern California. As
Stalinism swept through Eastern Europe, he attached himself to
the cause of anti-Communism with a determination that he carried into every campaign, whether it was against Alger Hiss or
Harry Truman. Always an opportunist, he exploited the tensions
and fears of the Cold War to advance his career. On October 1,
1949, when the Communists took control of China, he and other
conservatives ripped into the Democrats and raised a question
that was to haunt the country's political dialogue for decades—
"Who lost China?" The implication, though simplistic, was politically devastating: it was the Democrats who had lost China, and
history had chosen Nixon to recover the loss. In 1972, as president, Nixon reopened relations with a China that was still ruled
by the same Communists. Never one to think small, he called his

visit "the week that changed the world." Twenty years later, he
was to ask a similar question: "Who lost Russia?"

Nixon (or news about him) seemed to pursue me into college
and graduate school. I was quietly studying history—American,
Russian, Chinese, European; and he was cutting a controversial
swath on Capitol Hill, progressing from the House of Representatives to the Senate. He joined the Eisenhower ticket in 1952, when
I began thinking about joining the Army during the Korean War.
He became vice-president of the United States; I became a private
first class in Army intelligence.

He was still vice-president when I returned to Harvard in 1955
in pursuit of a Ph.D.; still vice-president when I entered the State
Department in 1956 to serve as a diplomatic attaché at the U.S.
Embassy in Moscow; still vice-president when Edward R. Murrow hired me in 1957 as a writer/reporter (and potential Moscow
correspondent) for CBS News; still vice-president when I reported on his famous "kitchen debate" with Nikita Khrushchev
in 1959; still vice-president when I reopened the CBS News bureau in Moscow in May 1960 immediately after the shooting down
of the American U-2 spy plane; and still vice-president when I
covered the Soviet angle of his unsuccessful presidential campaign in 1960, reporting the odd fact, as it seemed to me at the
time, that the Communists preferred the conservative Nixon to
the liberal Kennedy.

When Nixon lost the California gubernatorial race in 1962, I
was still a Moscow correspondent. Defeated twice in two years,
Nixon promised to disappear into the sunset, another failed politician. It was a promise, like many others, that he did not keep. In
any case, Nixon seemed very far away. I was absorbed at the time
with covering the Cuban missile crisis.

In February 1963, I was assigned to a new beat in the Washington bureau of CBS News—that of diplomatic correspondent. It

was a beat that I was to cover (even after joining NBC in 1980) until May 1987, when I resigned to accept a professorship at Harvard. Up to that point diplomacy was not a story that was routinely covered by CBS News or any of the other networks. It was considered to be rather exotic. Only after the missile crisis did the need for a specialist in diplomatic reporting become clear. It was new and exciting terrain, and I had a front-row seat.

As a journalist, I covered many summits, from Eisenhower and Khrushchev to Reagan and Gorbachev, Secretaries of State from Dulles to Shultz, foreign trips and conferences, negotiations about Vietnam and the Middle East, and an assortment of leaders from de Gaulle and Adenauer to Mitterand and Kohl. In other words, I covered a panoply of issues, personalities, and policies that would have interested Nixon. Though I covered him as vice-president and later as president, I never had the feeling that I knew Nixon as anything other than a remote and complex politician. I had never actually met him, never shaken hands with him, never dined with him, never exchanged a word with him.

For a time, during the mid-1960s, he fell off my radar screen entirely. I was absorbed with Vietnam, he with another run for the presidency. An intriguing article he wrote for *Foreign Affairs* in 1967 reawakened my interest in Nixon. He recommended "triangular diplomacy"—the use of China as diplomatic leverage on Russia to help win the war in Vietnam. This strategy was eye-catching, and after his close presidential victory in 1968 he moved to implement it—with costly results. I was one of hundreds of Washington-based journalists who covered his rise and observed his fall. His presidency was a portrait of peaks and valleys, the promise of great accomplishments sullied by a twisted set of personal and political values.

My attitude toward Nixon, and toward most other politicians, for that matter, was decidedly aloof. I felt that some distance between a journalist and a source was advisable. But in Washington, D.C., where journalists and politicians attended the same parties, prayed in the same churches or synagogues, and sent their children to the same schools, this was a ground rule, for many of us, that was often difficult to follow. "Inside the Beltway" represented a special way of life.

With Nixon, though, it was not difficult to maintain this distance. He treated the press with contempt, he held infrequent news conferences, and he lived so lonely a life that it seemed as if he had converted the Oval Office into an underground bunker. At the time I half suspected that, so far as Nixon and his immediate staff were concerned, I was not among their favorite journalists. In and of itself, this was not professionally disabling. I did my job; they did theirs.

Presidential displeasure was no novelty for me. During the Vietnam War, Lyndon Johnson had complained about my reporting. Once he actually telephoned and angrily accused me of damaging the security interests of the nation. At the other end of the line, I was left momentarily shaken. Had I in fact broadcast such sensitive information? Could I really have damaged the nation? The following day, having played the bad cop, Johnson decided to play the good one. He arranged for one of his top aides to leak an important story to me.

John Kennedy had also complained, on one occasion calling CBS Vice-President Blair Clark, one of his Harvard classmates, to criticize my analysis of his trip to Latin America in the spring of 1963.

Nixon himself never called reporters or their employers. He simply scribbled memos of rage, ordering his aides to deny access to CBS, the *New York Times,* or the *Washington Post*. He was to do worse, as I was personally to find out, much worse. It was not until the late spring of 1973, during the buildup of the Watergate crisis, that I became aware of the fact that Nixon had turned his fury—and the power of the U.S. government—against me. Why?

The evidence suggests that my trouble with Nixon started with a 1969 springtime decision by the Nixon administration to begin bombing North Vietnamese sanctuaries in Cambodia, which was then theoretically a neutral country. The justification was that the Communists were using Cambodia to transport men and matériel into South Vietnam.

The operation was "top secret." While the United States was in fact starting a program of troop withdrawals, the bombing of Cambodia might have come through to the administration's numerous critics as proof that the United States was really expanding the war.

I reported aspects of the story on radio and television, but it was William Beecher, who was then covering national security for the *New York Times,* who broke it with much greater force and in much greater detail on the front page, lower right-hand corner, on May 9, 1969. It was the kind of story that typically drove Nixon and his national security adviser, Henry Kissinger, to the edge of despair. They imagined leaks gushing from every corner of the bureaucracy; yet they knew that, aside from the Cambodians and the Vietnamese, only a few trusted aides were even aware of the Cambodia bombing. Who, then, was leaking? Who were the "traitors"? Even more important, in their minds, how could the ship of state navigate in such treacherous waters if secrets, hatched in the relative isolation of the White House basement, found their way so quickly to the front page of the *Times?* From these questions flowed a series of dreadful decisions that led ultimately to Watergate and the collapse of the Nixon presidency.

Within a matter of months, seventeen Americans were wiretapped in a feverish White House drive to find the leaker, or leakers. Thirteen of them worked in senior positions in the Nixon administration. Each had a "top secret" clearance. The other four were journalists; I was one of the four along with Beecher and Hedrick Smith of the *New York Times* and Henry Brandon of the London *Sunday Times.*

While Kissinger instigated most of these wiretaps, often to prove his leak-proof loyalty to Chief of Staff Bob Haldeman and others at the White House, Nixon ordered mine. This was to be the first in a series of actions that I was to learn about only a few years later. They included wiretapping my home phone, impugning my patriotism, adding me to an "enemies list," misusing the Internal Revenue Service to intimidate me and my family, and twice breaking into my office.

First, the story of the wiretap. On September 9, 1969, according to an FBI memorandum released by the Senate Foreign Relations Committee on June 11, 1973, Director J. Edgar Hoover sent a file on me to Attorney General John Mitchell, apparently on the assumption, which proved to be accurate, that Mitchell would then give it to Nixon. I never learned what was in the file, but Hoover had acquired a well-earned reputation for feeding titillating gossip, rumor, utter nonsense, and, one must assume, even confirmed information—what the experts would call "hard intelligence"—to a succession of grateful presidents. He had organized a Rube Goldberg, pre-computer-age file card system, filled with often unreliable, unevaluated, unchecked information, into which he would dip for excitement whenever he felt the need.

For example, on one occasion, in early May 1969, Hoover told Nixon that the White House had been "infected" by a "coterie of homosexuals at the highest levels." Nixon adored gossip. Who specifically? he asked. H. R. Haldeman, John Ehrlichman, and Dwight Chapin, came Hoover's astonishing response. (Haldeman and Ehrlichman, crewcut conservatives from California, were Nixon's closest White House aides. Chapin was Nixon's appointments secretary. All three later served prison terms because of their involvement in the Watergate scandal.) And who conveyed this information? A reporter, Hoover replied (Ehrlichman, *Witness to Power*, Simon & Schuster, p. 159). This was one example of Hoover's rantings, but Nixon did not choose to challenge the FBI director, who was himself suspected of being a homosexual, because he appreciated Hoover's infinite capacity for malicious meddling.

I had always assumed that I had a fat FBI file. I had been cleared for "top secret" work in Army Intelligence and the State Department. In addition, as a diplomatic correspondent, working at the height of the Cold War, I covered many national security stories and met or talked on the phone with dozens of senior American officials and diplomats representing many countries, including Communist ones. On occasion, my wife and I entertained such officials and diplomats at our home, often in the line of work but sometimes for the sheer pleasure of their company.

What then happened, according to the FBI memorandum, was that Nixon ordered Hoover to have an "immediate electronic surveillance [wiretap] put on this man." Through the attorney general's good offices, Nixon also told Hoover that "this of course should be 'accompanied by the other business.'"

Cartha D. De Loach, one of Hoover's top aides, asked Mitchell if, by "the other business," the president meant "physical surveillance," in addition to the wiretapping. Yes, Mitchell answered. De Loach said that such surveillance would require six men on a twenty-four-hour-a-day basis, which he thought would be a very expensive and inefficient proposition. Mitchell pondered De Loach's reservations "and then stated he thought the electronic surveillance would be sufficient at this time." Was it possible that Mitchell thought Nixon was overreacting to Hoover's file on me?

De Loach quickly sent Mitchell's request to Clyde Tolson, Hoover's closest assistant, and the FBI director then told the attorney general in a follow-up memorandum that the wiretap would be placed on my home phone in Chevy Chase, Maryland, "upon receipt of your written approval." Hoover added, carefully underlining his concern about wiretapping a prominent journalist, "In view of the sensitive nature of this investigation, no record is being made concerning the coverage and it is requested that this memorandum be returned upon approval." In fact, there was a "record" of the "coverage."

With the cooperation of the Chesapeake and Potomac Telephone Company, the "electronic surveillance" was secretly installed on my home phone on September 10, 1969. If one is to believe the FBI memorandum, it was lifted on November 4, 1969. It proved to be a total waste of time, effort, and money. If Nixon was seeking proof of national security leaks or conspiracies, what he got was a great deal of information about news schedules and car-pooling. My daughters were then six and almost four years of age, and arrangements had to be made to get them to and from school. According to David Wise's superbly researched book, *The American Police State,* "The summary of the FBI's wiretaps on Kalb . . . reads as follows: 'Reports were sent to Attorney-General Mitchell on October 9, 1969 and to the President on October 10, 1969 with respect to electronic surveillance of the residence of Mr. M [Kalb], a newsman. The summaries reported only personal family matters, news coverage of future events, and a discussion of criticism of the President by the media. None of the summaries reported on discussions of classified material'" (pp. 62–63).

The bugging operation, which was illegal (no judge ever cleared it), was conducted in total secrecy. I knew from my years in Moscow that dictatorships wiretapped their citizens, and, in the midst of the Cold War, I was even prepared to believe that democracies resorted to such techniques in extreme cases. By no stretch of the imagination was I such a case.

I learned nothing about the bugging until June 1973, when I received a call from John Crewdson, a reporter for the *New York Times*. He asked if I had ever covered the North Vietnamese in Paris. Yes, I replied. "You're the guy," Crewdson said. "You're the one they bugged." I asked Crewdson if, before writing his story, he could please double-check his information. A few minutes later, Crewdson called back. "You're the guy," he repeated.

Though on a good day the Kalb family considered itself to be sophisticated about the ways of the world, we were still shocked when we got the news. Why would our home phone be tapped? In Moscow, yes, but in Chevy Chase, Maryland? We searched our files, our calendars; I reviewed many of my broadcasts from Paris and Washington. What had I done to trigger Nixon's paranoia? During one dinnertime conversation, my children raised a sad question: how could they ever again respect the president? I suggested that they respect the presidency. By that time, they had known of only two presidents: Johnson, whom they associated with Vietnam, and Nixon, whom they associated with Watergate and then wiretaps.

In late 1974, I told David Wise in a taped interview: "We were personally, and as Americans, deeply offended that a president could resort to that kind of activity without a real justification. I would like to believe that if a president of the United States intrudes into your privacy, running against every tradition in this country, he has a very good reason for doing so. But in all of my research I came upon no reason" (interview between Wise and Kalb, December 20, 1974).

Part of my problem then was that I could not imagine the depths of Nixon's paranoia, nor could I grasp the extent of his hostility toward the press. As Watergate unraveled, I began to learn more about his ways. Not only did he wiretap my home; he also *questioned my loyalty.*

I can pinpoint the exact date. On November 3, 1969, Nixon requested prime time on network television to report on Vietnam. He wanted to undercut the antiwar movement, which was then planning a massive demonstration in Washington, and he wanted to underline the theme of Communist intransigence in the Paris peace talks. As was customary at the time, several hours before the president spoke, the White House distributed copies of his speech and an exchange of letters, both embargoed for delivery, between Nixon and the North Vietnamese leader, Ho Chi Minh, and arranged a Kissinger backgrounder for diplomatic reporters.

Obviously Kissinger put his best spin on the speech. Few briefers were better at the job. Still, having heard his pitch and read the speech and the exchange between Nixon and Ho, I thought that the president had overstated the degree of Ho's intransigence. I sensed some flexibility. It was late in the afternoon when Kissinger finished, and I still had a few hours to check with other administration experts before Nixon would speak on television. A few of them told me that, far from rejecting the president's overture, Ho seemed, by Hanoi's usually rigid standards, to be opening the door to a possible compromise. One or two even went so far as to express surprise that the president had been so negative—unless, of course, he himself did not want a compromise. "The obstacle," Nixon said in his speech, "is the other side's absolute refusal to show the least willingness to join us in seeking a just peace" (Donovan and Shearer, *Unsilent Revolution,* p. 115).

In those days, CBS gloried in a journalistic practice that was later dubbed "instant analysis." Immediately after a presidential speech, the network would arrange for a small group of informed correspondents to fill in the half hour or hour of unused air time with analysis of the speech or event. If, for example, the president spoke for twenty-two minutes, CBS would set aside approximately eight minutes for analysis. The Nixon White House would often object to the analysis, arguing that it interfered with the president's message. The tension between the networks and the White House was palpable. On this particular evening, moderator Dan Rather asked for my analysis of the president's speech.

Pointing at the television camera, I said: "It was aimed, as the president put it, at you, the great silent majority . . . presumably those who do not demonstrate, those who want an honorable end of the war but have difficulty defining what an honorable end is and are willing to trust the president to get it. Those who are not so willing will point out the absence of a new announcement on troop withdrawals or a definite timetable for total withdrawal of U.S. forces, and they may disagree with the president's judgment that the Ho Chi Minh letter was a flat rejection of his own letter. The Ho Chi Minh letter contained, it seems, some of the softest, most accommodating language found in a Communist document concerning the war in Vietnam in recent years."

My analysis, as it turned out, led to two major decisions, one by the government and one by CBS, that soured relations between the government and the networks for a long time. The government acted first. On November 13, 1969, Vice-President Spiro Agnew unleashed a stinging attack on network news, in the process attacking me, though not by name. "One commentator twice contradicted the president's statement about the exchange of correspondence with Ho Chi Minh," Agnew said. The vice-president then described the three networks as nothing more than liberal think tanks, filled with "nattering nabobs of negativism," "elites," "effete intellectuals" from the Northeast engaged in "querulous criticism." There was an undercurrent of anti-Semitism, and unfortunately Agnew's attack struck a responsive chord among many Americans.

The White House added to the Agnew attack by threatening to toughen government regulation of the networks. CBS feared that the newly appointed head of the Federal Communications Commission, Dean Burch, would cancel or rearrange radio and television licenses. Millions of dollars hung in the balance. In addition, Nixon aides visited CBS headquarters in New York to complain about Dan Rather's reporting from the White House.

In 1973, after years of threats and warnings from the Nixon administration, CBS caved to the pressure while insisting that nothing had happened. Chairman William Paley decided to drop "instant analysis." A number of us in the CBS Washington bureau, including Roger Mudd, George Herman, and Daniel Schorr, objected strenuously to the Paley decision in a letter to the chairman. We argued that Paley's decision set a terrible precedent. In our view, it encouraged the government to believe that the networks could indeed be intimidated into changing their editorial practices. Strained negotiations followed, but basically we failed to change Paley's mind. And though, after a while, "instant analysis" was to return in various guises from time to time, it never again recaptured its free spirit and independence. Governmental Agnewism had triumphed.

Two days after the president's speech about Vietnam, on the morning of November 5, 1969, Nixon met with his key advisers, including Haldeman, Kissinger, Chapin, spokesman Ronald Ziegler, communications chief Herb Klein, speechwriters Pat Buchanan and Ray Price, and newcomer Jeb Magruder. Nixon was described as feisty. The "silent majority" had responded enthusiastically to his appeal, and the antiwar movement was put on the defensive. Magruder, in his book, *An American Life,* caught the president's mood. "We've got those liberal bastards on the run now, he was telling us in a proud monologue; we've got them on the run and we're going to keep them on the run. . . . In politics, he said, the best defense was a good offense; we'd floored those liberal sons of bitches with the TV speech and we'd never let them get back on their feet" (p. 53).

Nixon turned to Buchanan. "How were the television reports last night?" (It was actually the evening before.)

"They were all good except one," Buchanan replied. Then, according to Magruder, he named a "network correspondent who we felt often showed an anti-Administration bias."[1]

Magruder's account continued:

"Henry Kissinger broke in.

"'Well, Mr. President, that man is an agent of the Rumanian government.'

"He explained that the correspondent was on a retainer to provide Washington reports to the Rumanian government, which is, of course, a Communist government.

"'That's right,' the President said angrily. 'That guy is a Communist.'

"He looked at me.

"'Jeb, you're our new ramrod around here. Get the word out on that guy.'. . .

"I had received a direct order from the President to get the word out on the television correspondent's alleged ties to the Rumanian government," wrote Magruder. "I didn't waste any time in soul-searching."

---

1. In the CD-ROM version of *The Haldeman Diaries*, Haldeman identified me as one of the two network correspondents whose reporting on this occasion angered the White House. The other was Bill Lawrence of ABC News ("Nightline" transcript, May 16, 1994, p. 3). This reference does not appear in the printed book.

Preposterous as the charge was, when it was uttered by a president it took on a serious dimension. White House aides echoed the line. Stephen Hess, who worked for Nixon at the time, chanced upon Klein in the White House one day. Knowing that Hess and I were friends, Klein told him that he ought to know that the president had said that I was "a Rumanian agent." Stunned, Hess called me with the information. Magruder drew a single lesson from Nixon's charge—not that he should try to find out whether it was right or wrong, but that if Nixon said Kalb was "a Rumanian agent," then he was "a Rumanian agent." "There just wasn't any room for debate on the issue," Magruder wrote. "The media were out to get us, so we'd get them first" (p. 55).

The timing of this meeting was interesting. It suggested that the White House was not exactly functioning like a Swiss watch. Here was Nixon in a mood to "floor those liberal sons of bitches," and yet, according to FBI records, he (or someone, like Mitchell, acting in his name) ordered the removal of my wiretap the day before he opened his "Rumania" attack against me. The tap was lifted on November 4, 1969. The meeting took place on the morning of November 5, 1969. One would have imagined that if Nixon really thought that I was "a Rumanian agent," he would have had even more reason to keep the wiretap in place. By allowing it to be removed, however, Nixon might have been indicating that even though he did not believe I was a foreign agent, or had no "proof" to that effect, he still wanted to make my life difficult. Or it was possible that Mitchell operated on one wavelength and Nixon on another, and coordination between the two was loose or even nonexistent.

A few years later, after I had heard about Nixon's "Rumania" accusation, I checked with Kissinger and he indignantly denied that he had ever raised the subject. His denial never wavered. Finally, many years later, in a letter to me dated August 21, 1992, he wrote: "I am amazed that you should ask about the preposterous Rumanian spy allegation which I thought I had laid to rest years ago. My answer is still the same: it is absurd. I have always considered you one of the ablest and fairest journalists."

One of Kissinger's aides offered a variation on the theme of absurdity. He said that in Nixon's White House there was so much cursing, so much of the most vile language in constant use, that "Rumanian agent" came to be bandied about as the equivalent of "press prick," one of Nixon's favorite expletives.

The third string on Nixon's bow was *his use of the IRS to intimidate reporters.*

On October 17, 1969, Magruder proposed to Haldeman that the administration "utilize the Internal Revenue Service as a method to look into the various organizations that we are most concerned about." In time, I learned that it was not only "organizations" but individuals whom Nixon targeted for special abuse. Within a year, the IRS ordered a full-scale audit of my income tax return. Preparation for such an audit could be a major disruption in any household. So it was in ours. It took weeks to produce receipts and documentation for every claimed deduction or expenditure. Accountants' bills skyrocketed. The audit, when it was finally done, proved to be a total vindication. Not a nickel was either requested or returned.

And so it went for several years. We were frequently audited, we had to go through elaborate preparations for each audit, and not once was there a problem. When I asked the IRS why we were being audited, we never got a satisfactory answer. Only in 1977, through the kind intercession of Washington attorney Lloyd Cutler, did I learn that the audits had initially been ordered by the White House, which is what I had suspected, and that they had recurred because our name was flagged in the IRS computer for an annual check.

There was more—*enemies lists.* On August 16, 1971, White House counsel John Dean, who later broke with Nixon and described Watergate as a "cancer" on his presidency, compiled the first of a rolling series of "enemies lists." From sympathetic souls, such as Buchanan, he got recommendations: Democrats on Capitol Hill who opposed the president's policy on Vietnam, and reporters and editors who criticized the president. Critics became enemies, and criticism became treason in the Nixon White House. A pervading sense of arrogance corrupted the president's men. They had power, and they intended to use it against their critics, whom they saw as "enemies of the people," of the "silent majority" who supported the president. Like "enemies" of any authoritarian system, they had to be squashed and silenced. Dean intended to use "available federal machinery" against these enemies. On behalf of the president, he wanted to "give a hard time" to "our political enemies."

In July 1974, during the House impeachment hearings, I learned that I was on Nixon's "enemies list." It proved to be a badge of honor, for among Nixon's "enemies," in addition to Washington politicians and journalists, were a broad range of impressive Americans, including Harvard president Derek Bok, actor Paul Newman, and quarterback Joe Namath.

It turned out that giving a "hard time" to the administration's political "enemies" included *ransacking my CBS office.* It was a small broadcast booth at the State Department overlooking a large auditorium. Twice, during the summer of 1973, it was broken into and ransacked. On the weekend of July 7–8, at the same time that Potomac Associates, a Washington think tank run by William Watts, a former Foreign Service officer who had worked on Kissinger's NSC staff at the Nixon White House, reported a break-in, I discovered that my State Department office had been searched. "It looked like a cyclone had hit the place," I later told David Wise (interview, December 20, 1974). "Clearly, somebody had gone through it." There were no important papers in the office, only press releases and speech texts, but I reported the incident to State Department security.

Two weeks later, as Potomac Associates was again burglarized, my State Department office was again searched. "It was messed up, but not as bad." I told Wise, "I complained again, and they put a lock on the door."

Why would someone break into my State Department office, twice? At the time my brother, Bernard, and I were researching a biography of Kissinger. Could the burglars have been looking for evidence that would have incriminated Kissinger in the leaking of classified information to us? He did give us carefully selected information in the course of several interviews. We had the impression throughout that he cooperated because he wanted to enhance his image as the key figure in devising U.S. foreign policy. But to the best of my knowledge, what he gave us was not classified. I told Wise, "I had a lot of Kissinger tapes and transcripts for the book, but they were at my home, not at the State Department." (Shortly after the break-ins, I installed a burglar alarm system at my home, not against the possibility of an ordinary burglary but against the likelihood of an administration-inspired break-in. At the time this was not a farfetched notion. On White House orders, columnist Joseph Kraft's home in Georgetown was burglarized in an attempt either to install a tap on his phone or to steal "incriminating" information.)

The General Services Administration was responsible for State Department security. GSA spokespersons informed me that they had investigated the two break-ins but had no evidence, no leads. My colleague, the late Darius Jhabvala of the *Boston Globe,* who

had an office down the hall, told me that one quiet day he happened to see two people going through my office papers. He said
that they were wearing GSA uniforms. I asked the GSA for an
explanation. A spokesperson insisted that the GSA would never
break into any reporter's office. On reflection, the spokesperson
was probably right. The GSA wouldn't have done it, but officials
with keys to government buildings or hired outsiders wearing
GSA uniforms could well have been the ones who broke into my
CBS office at the State Department. In this context, I often
thought about the Watergate break-in. Only that time, the burglars were caught.

All of these memories of "enemies lists" and wiretaps, of
Nixon and Watergate, returned to me with a special force in the
spring of 1992, as I pursued my research on the Nixon memo. At
the time what quickly became clear was that an interview with
Nixon would be helpful—not essential but certainly helpful. But
would Nixon talk to me? Daniel Schorr, who had himself incurred
Nixon's wrath during Watergate, once told me that he did not
mind "making up" with Nixon, because he—Schorr—did not
have an "enemies list." I did not, either. I figured that if Nixon
would talk to me about his efforts on behalf of Russian aid—what
his associate, Dimitri Simes, described as "the major cause in his
life"—then I would be pleased to incorporate his views into my
report.

In late April 1992, I telephoned William Safire and asked
whether he thought Nixon would give me an interview. My idea
was that Safire had a direct pipeline to Nixon and that, if anyone
could help me get through to the former president, it would be
Safire. "Call him," Safire advised. "These days, you can never tell."

On April 28, 1992, I called Nixon's office in New Jersey and
spoke with someone who suggested that I put my request in writing to Kathy O'Connor, one of Nixon's assistants.

My letter read:

Dear Ms. O'Connor:

I am doing research on the question of American aid to Russia—and most specifically on the role played in President Bush's decision by President Nixon's memo. My initial inquiries suggest that the Nixon memo played a very significant role indeed.

During a discussion with my friend, Bill Safire, I said that it would be wonderful if President Nixon would discuss this matter with me but that I doubted that he would. Bill said, well, try; you can never tell.

I am trying. I know that I shall be in the New York area from June 18 through June 21 doing research on this theme. Would it be possible for me to visit with President Nixon during this time period or some other and learn from him what he intended and what he thinks he has achieved with respect to his memo on American aid to Russia? I'd be prepared, of course, to go to his office or his home.

Thank you for your consideration,
Sincerely yours,
Marvin Kalb

The letter was on Harvard University stationery, and my status as a professor was unmistakable. In other words, it was clear that I was no longer a journalist.

On May 3, 1992, after a number of unanswered telephone calls, I received a brief written response from Ms. O'Connor. "Thanks for your letter of April 28th," it began. "Unfortunately, President Nixon's calendar is fully committed through the fall—including some extensive travel plans—and it will not be possible for him to meet with you at this time. He asked, however, that I pass on to you his appreciation and very best wishes."

How was I to read the Nixon response? Certainly the note was courteous, but it seemed to be saying that for the foreseeable future ("through the fall") he didn't have the time to see me. I called Safire for an interpretation. Safire didn't even have to look into his tea leaves. "He doesn't want to see you," he said flatly. Why? "Because," he continued, "he thinks you'll depict him as manipulative."

"Nixon? Manipulative?" I responded.

On May 28, 1992, I dispatched another letter to Ms. O'Connor. If he would not talk to me, maybe he would write to me. My letter read, in part:

> Dear Ms. O'Connor:
>
> I was of course sorry to learn from your faxed letter of May 3, 1992 that Mr. Nixon would not be able to see me. . . .
>
> Since an interview is not possible, do you think that Mr. Nixon might be willing to answer a few questions in writing, the answers to be used only in connection with this research? I shall take the liberty of asking the questions, and I'd be grateful for his answers. If this approach is equally unsatisfactory, then I request only that you so inform me and I thank you for your time.

I then listed five questions:

1. What were your basic differences with the President on the question of aid to Russia?
2. Why did you write the memo?
3. Why did you feel the need to send it to 50 friends and colleagues? (Was it exactly 50, or about 50? And did they go out in one wave or two?)
4. Did you expect the memo to leak?

5. Was your conference, which opened on March 11, 1992, always intended to be a Washington platform for your explicit critique of the President's aid policy, or was the timing coincidental?

I never heard from Ms. O'Connor, Nixon, or anyone else in his entourage. I did not need Safire to interpret the silence. The question of aid to Russia might well have been the paramount issue of his life, but even after all these years, Nixon must still have considered me an "enemy."

THE NIXON MEMO (MARCH 1992)

HOW TO LOSE THE COLD WAR

While the candidates have addressed scores of significant issues in the presidential campaign, the most important issue since the end of World War II—the fate of the political and economic reforms in Russia—has been virtually ignored. As a result, the United States and the West risk snatching defeat in the cold war from the jaws of victory.

We have heard repeatedly that the cold war has ended and that the West has won it. This is only half true. The Communists have lost the cold war, but the West has not yet won it. Communism collapsed because its ideas failed. Today, the ideas of freedom are on trial. If they fail to produce a better life in Russia and the other former Soviet republics, a new and more dangerous despotism will take power, with the people trading freedom for security and entrusting their future to old hands with new faces.

We are at a watershed moment in history. The historical significance of the democratic revolution in the Soviet Union compares only with events like the defeat of Napoleon at Waterloo in 1815, the Versailles Peace Conference in 1919, and the creation of NATO and the Marshall Plan in 1948. A century of stability in Europe, the drift toward World War II in the 1920's and 1930's, and a half century of successful containment of the Soviet Union were all determined by how the statesmen of the major powers responded to these critical moments. While opportunities and dangers on that same order of magnitude face us today, the West has failed so far to seize the moment to shape the history of the next half century.

Russia is the key to success. It is there that the final battle of the cold war will be won or lost. The stakes could not be higher. If freedom succeeds in Russia—if President Yeltsin's economic reforms succeed in creating a successful free-market economy—the future will hold the promise of reduced spending on arms, cooperation in coping with crises around the world, and economic growth through expanded international trade. More important, freedom's success will reverberate in the world's last isolated strongholds of Communism—North Korea, Cuba, Vietnam, and China. Their leaders will face irresistible pressures to take the first steps toward political reform.

If Yeltsin fails, the prospects for the next fifty years will turn grim. The Russian people will not turn back to Communism. But a new, more dangerous despotism based on extremist Russian nationalism will take power. We must remember that even before Communism, Russia had an expansionist tradition dating back seven centuries. The leaders of a new despotism, who have already been organizing themselves to take over in the event that Yeltsin's reforms fail, will stoke nationalist passions and exploit the tendency of the Russian people to turn to the strong hand—even to dictatorship—during times of trouble.

If a new despotism prevails, everything gained in the great peaceful revolution of 1991 will be lost. War could break out in the former Soviet Union as the new despots use force to restore the "historical borders" of Russia. The new East European democracies would be imperiled. China's totalitarians would breath a sigh of relief. The new Russian regime—whose leaders would cozy up to the Soviet Union's former clients in Iraq, Syria, Libya, and North Korea—would threaten our interests in hot spots around the world. It would sell conventional weapons, ballistic

missiles, and nuclear technology to any buyer. A new Russian despotism inspired by imperial nationalism shorn of the baggage of
the dying faith of Communism would be even more dangerous
than Soviet totalitarianism.

If freedom fails in Russia, we will see the tide of freedom that
has been sweeping over the world begin to ebb, and dictatorship
rather than democracy will be the wave of the future.

In light of the stakes involved, the West must do everything it
can to help President Yeltsin succeed. Yeltsin has been maligned
by friends of freedom in the West who should have known better.
Some say that he is not democratic enough politically, others that
he is not smart enough intellectually, and still others that he is not
smooth enough socially. A few who dismissed him as a boob in
the past now seem to be hoping for his failure so that they can
claim to have been proved right. That thinking is not worthy of
the world's only superpower.

Like all strong leaders who try to make a difference, Yeltsin is
not perfect. He has made serious mistakes. But he is an extraordinary historic figure. He is the first Russian leader in history to be
chosen through free elections. Unlike Gorbachev, he has irrevocably repudiated socialism as well as Communism. He risked his life
in facing down a gang of card-carrying killers in the coup attempt
in August 1991. He recognized the independence of the Baltic
states and the other republics of the former Soviet Union. He
abandoned the Russian imperial tradition—throwing away the
keys of what Lenin called the "jailhouse of nations"—by dissolv-
ing the Soviet Union and forging the voluntary Commonwealth
of Independent States. He risked his enormous popularity by embarking on painful free-market economic reforms, including the
indispensable first step of allowing astronomical price rises. He
has moved decisively toward privatization of Soviet enterprises
and decollectivization of Soviet agriculture, steps Gorbachev re-

fused even to consider. He has completely cut off the $15 billion in foreign aid and trade subsidies that Gorbachev in his 1990 budget continued to provide to Cuba and other anti-America Communist losers in the developing world. He has not only matched but exceeded the cuts in nuclear weapons proposed by President Bush.

The bottom line is that Yeltsin is the most pro-Western leader of Russia in history. Moreover, whatever his flaws, the alternative of new despotism would be infinitely worse.

What has the United States and the West done so far to help Russia's first democratic, free-market oriented, non-expansionist government? We have provided credits for the purchase of agricultural products. We have held a photo-opportunity international conference of fifty-seven foreign secretaries that was long on rhetoric but short on action. We are sending sixty cargo-planes of surplus food and medical supplies leftover from the Persian Gulf War. We have decided to send two hundred Peace Corps volunteers—a generous action if the target of our aid were a small country like Upper Volta but mere tokenism if applied to Russia, a nation of almost 200 million people covering one-seventh of the world's landmass. This is a pathetically inadequate response in light of the opportunities and dangers we face in crisis in the former Soviet Union.

What is to be done? To meet the moment, the West must step up to the task of helping President Yeltsin's government in six crucial ways:

—We must provide humanitarian food and medical aid to get Russia through the critical months until Yeltsin's reforms have a chance to start working.

—We must create a "free enterprise corps" that will send thousands of Western managers to Russia to infuse newly independent enterprises with free-market know-how.

—We must reschedule Soviet debt incurred during the Gorbachev era and defer interest payments until the new market economy begins to function.

—We must allow greater access to Western markets for Russia's exports.

—We must be ready to join with others to provide tens of billions of dollars for currency stabilization through the IMF or other means as soon as Russia reins in the growth of its money supply.

—We must create a single Western-led organization to assess Soviet needs and coordinate wide-ranging governmental and private aid projects, as the United States did when embarking on the rebuilding of Western Europe after World War II.

In light of the depth of the Russian economic crisis, there is no time to lose. Those who would put off major action on these fronts until the next international aid conference in July 1992 could find that this is too little and too late.

Can we afford these initiatives? As Herb Stein has pointed out, "The United States is a very rich nation. We are not rich enough to do everything, but we are rich enough to do everything important." Forty-three years ago, the United States alone helped its allies and enemies in Europe and Japan recover from World War II. A strong case can be made that the United States has carried the burden of foreign aid and world leadership for long enough and that it is time for Europe and Japan to assume the major financial burden in helping Russia and the other former Soviet republics. But the United States as the strongest and richest nation in the world must provide the leadership.

At the same time, we must be willing to bear our share of the burden. To play in this game, we must have a seat at the table. To get a seat at the table, we must be ready to put some chips in the pot. The stakes are high, and we are playing as if it were a penny ante game.

It is a tough call politically. Opinion polls indicate that foreign policy rates only in the single digits among issues that voters consider to be important. The American people overwhelmingly oppose all foreign aid because they want to see that money spent on solving our problems at home. But the mark of great political leadership is not simply to support what is popular but to make what is unpopular popular if that serves America's national interest. In addition, what seems politically profitable in the short term may prove costly in the long term. The hot-button issue in the 1950's was, "Who lost China?" If Yeltsin goes down, the question of "who lost Russia" will be an infinitely more devastating issue in the 1990's.

Those who oppose aid argue that charity begins at home. I agree. But aid to Russia and other reformist republics of the former Soviet Union is not charity. We must recognize that what helps us abroad helps us at home. If Yeltsin is replaced by a new aggressive Russian nationalist, we can kiss the peace dividend good-bye. Not only would the world become more dangerous, but our defense and foreign policies would also become far more expensive. Tinkering with the tax code or launching domestic initiatives will have little economic significance if the new hostile despotism in Russia forces the West to rearm. On the positive side, if Yeltsin succeeds, a free-market Russia will provide an opportunity for billions of dollars in trade, which will create millions of jobs in the United States. Most important, a democratic Russia would be a non-expansionist Russia, freeing our children and grandchildren in the next century of the fear of armed conflict because democracies do not start wars.

President Bush is uniquely qualified to meet this challenge. The brilliant leadership he demonstrated in mobilizing the coalition abroad and the American people at home to win victory in the Persian Gulf War can ensure that the cold war will not end just with the defeat of Communism but also with the victory of freedom.

Abramson, Jeffrey B., F. Christopher Arterton, and Gary R. Orren.
1988. *The Electronic Commonwealth*. New York: Basic Books.
Ambrose, Stephen E. 1987. *Nixon*. Vol. 1: *The Education of a Politician,
1913–1962;* vol. 2: *The Triumph of a Politician, 1962–1972;* vol. 3: *Ruin and
Recovery, 1973–1990*. New York: Simon & Schuster.
Barone, Michael. 1990. *Our Country*. New York: Free Press.
Bernstein, Carl, and Bob Woodward. 1974. *All the President's Men*. New
York: Simon & Schuster.
Beschloss, Michael. 1992. "How Nixon Came In from the Cold." *Vanity
Fair,* June.
Broder, David S. 1980. *Changing of the Guard: Power and Leadership in
America*. New York: Simon & Schuster.
Destler, I. M., Leslie H. Gelb, and Anthony Lake. 1984. *Our Own Worst
Enemy: The Unmaking of American Foreign Policy*. New York: Simon &
Schuster.
Donovan, Robert J., and Ray Scherer. 1992. *Unsilent Revolution: Television
News and American Public Life, 1948–1991*. New York: Cambridge
University Press.
Drew, Elizabeth. 1974. *Washington Journal: The Events of 1973–1974*. New
York: Random House.
Ehrlichman, John. 1982. *Witness to Power: The Nixon Years*. New York:
Simon & Schuster.
Evans, Rowland, Jr., and Robert D. Novak. 1971. *Nixon in the White
House: The Frustration of Power*. New York: Random House.
Goodwin, Doris Kearns. 1977. *Lyndon Johnson and the American Dream*.
New York: American Library.
Haig, Alexander M., Jr., with Charles McCarry. 1992. *Inner Circles: How
America Changed the World*. New York: Warner Books.
Haldeman, H. R. 1994. *The Haldeman Diaries: Inside the Nixon White
House*. New York: G. P. Putnam's Sons.
Hersh, Seymour M. 1992. "Nixon's Last Cover-Up: The Tapes He
Wants the Archives to Suppress." *New Yorker* 68:76–82, December
14.
Hess, Stephen. 1981. *The Washington Reporters*. Washington, D.C.:
Brookings Institution.

Hess, Stephen, and David S. Broder. 1967. *The Republican Establishment: The Present and Future of the G.O.P.* New York: Harper & Row.

Johnson, Lyndon Baines. 1971. *The Vantage Point: Perspectives of the Presidency, 1963–1969.* New York: Holt, Rinehart & Winston.

Joyce, Ed. 1988. *Prime Times, Bad Times.* New York: Doubleday.

Kalb, Marvin, and Bernard Kalb. 1974. *Kissinger.* Boston: Little, Brown.

Karnow, Stanley. 1983. *Vietnam: A History.* New York: Viking Press.

Kelly, Michael. 1993. "David Gergen, Master of the Game." *New York Times Magazine,* October 31, pp. 62–71.

Kissinger, Henry. 1979. *White House Years.* Boston: Little, Brown.

————. 1982. *Years of Upheaval.* Boston: Little, Brown.

Kutler, Stanley I. 1990. *The Wars of Watergate: The Last Crisis of Richard Nixon.* New York: Knopf.

Lemert, James B., William R. Elliott, James M. Bernstein, William L. Rosenberg, and Karl J. Nestvold. 1991. *News Verdicts, the Debates, and Presidential Campaigns.* New York: Praeger Publishers.

Magruder, Jeb Stuart. 1974. *An American Life: One Man's Road to Watergate.* New York: Atheneum.

Manchester, William. 1967. *The Death of a President.* New York: Harper & Row.

Mankiewicz, Frank. 1971. *Perfectly Clear: Nixon from Whittier to Watergate.* New York: Quadrangle/New York Times Book Co.

McCullough, David G. 1992. *Truman.* New York: Simon & Schuster.

McGinniss, Joe. 1969. *The Selling of the President, 1968.* New York: Trident.

Morris, Roger. 1990. *Richard Milhous Nixon: The Rise of an American Politician.* New York: Henry Holt & Company.

Neustadt, Richard E. 1990. *Presidential Power and the Modern Presidents: The Politics of Leadership from Roosevelt to Reagan.* New York: Free Press.

Newhouse, John. 1973. *Cold Dawn: The Story of SALT.* New York: Holt, Rinehart & Winston.

Nixon, Richard M. 1978. *RN: The Memoirs of Richard Nixon.* New York: Grosset & Dunlap.

————. 1982. *Leaders.* New York: Warner Books.

————. 1983. *Real Peace: A Strategy for the West.* New York: Richard Nixon.

————. 1985. *No More Vietnams.* New York: Arbor House.

————. 1988. *1999: Victory without War.* New York: Simon & Schuster.

————. 1990. *In the Arena: A Memoir of Victory, Defeat and Renewal.* New York: Simon & Schuster.

————. 1992. *Seize the Moment, America's Challenge in a One-Superpower World.* New York: Simon & Schuster.

————. 1994. *Beyond Peace*. New York: Random House.

Roberts, Chalmers M. 1973. *First Rough Draft*. New York: Praeger Publishers.

————. 1977. *The Washington Post: The First 100 Years*. Boston: Houghton Mifflin.

Sabato, Larry J. 1991. *Feeding Frenzy: How Journalism Has Transformed American Politics*. New York: Free Press.

Safire, William. 1968. *Before the Fall: An Inside View of the Pre-Watergate White House*. New York: Doubleday.

————. 1968. *The New Language of Politics*. New York: Random House.

————. 1978. *Safire's Political Dictionary*. New York: Random House.

————. 1980. *Safire's Washington*. New York: Times Books.

Schell, Jonathan. 1989. *Observing the Nixon Years*. New York: Pantheon Books.

Schlesinger, Arthur M., Jr. 1965. *A Thousand Days: John F. Kennedy in the White House*. Boston: Houghton Mifflin.

————. 1973. *The Imperial Presidency*. Boston: Houghton Mifflin.

————. 1978. *Robert Kennedy and His Times*. Boston: Houghton Mifflin.

Schorr, Daniel. 1977. *Clearing the Air*. Boston: Houghton Mifflin.

Smith, Geoffrey. 1991. *Reagan and Thatcher*. New York: Norton.

Sorenson, Theodore C. 1965. *Kennedy*. New York: Harper & Row.

Szulc, Tad. 1978. *The Illusion of Peace: Foreign Policy in the Nixon Years*. New York: Viking Press.

Taylor, Paul. 1990. *See How They Run: Electing the President in an Age of Mediaocracy*. New York: Alfred A. Knopf.

Ungar, Sanford. 1989. *The Papers & the Papers*. New York: Columbia University Press.

Valenti, Jack. 1975. *A Very Human President*. New York: W. W. Norton.

White, Theodore H. 1961. *The Making of the President, 1960*. New York: Atheneum House.

Wise, David. 1973. *The Politics of Lying*. New York: Random House.

————. 1976. *The American Police State: The Government against the People*. New York: Random House.

Woodward, Bob, and Carl Bernstein. 1976. *The Final Days*. New York: Simon & Schuster.

"How to Lose the Cold War," Nixon's memo of March 1992, is referred to as the
memo throughout this index; *"America's Role in the Emerging World,"* the conference associated with the memo, is referred to as the AREW conference.

icy of, 23–24, 26–29; meetings
with Gorbachev, 35–36; Nixon's criticism of, 28–29; at Nixon's funeral, 185–86; Nixon's
letter to, 23–24; relationship
with Nixon, 37–38, 155,
184–85; and Sadat's funeral, 25;
speaking style of, 102–3
Real Peace (Nixon), 28–29, 67
Real War (Nixon), 23
Rebozo, Charles G. ("Bebe"), 16
recession. *See* economy, in U.S.
Red Army, 38–39, 142, 166
Red Star, 165
reforms: in Eastern Europe,
119–20; of Gorbachev, 34; in
Russia, 1–2, 60, 68, 120, 124,
140, 151, 182, 217; in Soviet
Union, 1, 42–47; and Yeltsin,
61–64, 69, 73, 218, 220
Reich, Robert, 52
Remnick, David, 41, 97
Republican National Committee,
54, 118
Republican Party: "adopts" Truman, 100; after Goldwater's defeat, 12; and call for impeachment of Truman, 25; and
Checkers speech, 9; conference
of, 32; divisions of, 53, 83, 96,
114; National Convention of,
76; Nixon's appearance at fundraiser of, 19; 1952 ticket of,
8–9; and wiretapping, 16
Revere, Paul, 49
Richard Nixon Center for Peace
and Freedom, 160, 183
Richard Nixon Library and Birthplace, 32, 50, 95, 183, 186
right to privacy, and White House
tapes, 18

risk taking, 32
RN. *See* Nixon, Richard
RN: The Memoirs of Richard Nixon
(Nixon), 19–20
Rolling Stone (magazine), 31
Rollins, Edward, 23
Roosevelt, Eleanor, 145
Roosevelt, Franklin Delano, 33
Rosenblatt, Roger, 24, 138
Rosenfeld, Stephen S., 165
Rosenthal, A. M., 164
Rosenthal, Harry, 82
ruble, stabilization of, 63, 134
Rudman, Warren, 52, 97
Rumania, 207–9
Russian Republic: ability to absorb aid, 163–64; anti-
American sentiment in, 165–
66, 169, 175; coups in, 34–35,
71, 166–67, 171, 219; debts of,
142, 149, 158, 220; Duma of,
163, 170; economy of, 63, 136,
140–41, 143, 149, 176, 219; elections in, 43, 45–46, 62, 71, 167–
68, 176, 219; emergency plans
for aid in, 140–41, 153; exports
of, 73, 221; and free market
economic theories, 3, 33, 69,
161, 165; Liberal Democratic
Party in, 167; presidential election in, 45–46, 62, 71, 176, 219;
reforms in, 1–2, 60, 68, 120,
124, 140, 151, 182, 217; stabilization of currency in, 63, 73,
134, 221; U.S. policies toward,
5, 32–35, 59, 61–65, 162–66,
179; U.S. relations with, 35–37,
62–63, 144, 162–65, 169,
174–77; workers in, 149,
164. *See also* democratization;
foreign aid; Gorbachev, Mik-

Washington Post: and aid for Russia, 44, 163, 165; embarrassment of, 92; and investigation of Watergate, 15; Nixon denies access to, 198; and Nixon memo, 82–84, 90; and Nixon's death, 192; Nixon's memo discussed in, 83–85, 90, 92, 189–90; and Nixon's speeches by, 30; and Nixon/Yeltsin flap, 174; Simes's op-ed piece in, 178–79; and speeches, 115; "Who lost Russia?" column in, 105; and Yeltsin's U. N. trip, 62

Washington Times, 75, 82

Watergate: and coverup, 15–16, 32; effect of, on public attitudes, 6, 93, 97, 125, 144, 151, 162, 186, 193; effects of, on Nixon Cabinet, 50–51; and 1972 elections, 54; European attitude toward, 21; payoffs for, 15; and political rehabilitation, 3, 5, 22–23, 29–30, 33, 56, 77–78, 97, 109–10, 186; and possible impeachment, 2, 51, 83, 144, 210; Simes's interpretation of, 40; and White House tapes, 16–18, 18

Waterloo, 69, 217

Watts, William, 210

Weimar Republic, 119

White, Theodore H., 9, 23

White House Correspondents Association, 185

White House press corps, 14

White House tapes, 16–18

"Who's Hot" (column), 31

Wicker, Tom, 6

Wills, Garry, 9, 53–54

Wilson, Pete, 186

Wilson, Woodrow, 77

wiretaps: and coverage of bombing of Cambodia, 199–200; of Kalb's phone, 2, 199–203, 208, 212; in Watergate coverup, 15, 187

Wise, David, 202–3, 210–11

Wofford, Harris, 96

Woodward, Bob, 15, 57

World Bank, 133–34, 136

World War I, isolationism after, 119

World War II: aid for countries after, 73, 99–100, 117, 195, 221; aid for Soviet Union during, 101; reforms in Soviet Union after, 1; and U.S. isolationism, 119

Wye Plantation (Maryland), 85

Yale University, 53

Yardley, Jonathan, 192

Yasuda, Hiroshi, 134

Yavlinsky, Grigory, 42–45, 170, 176

Yeltsin, Boris: Clinton's support of, 167–68, 181–82; compared to Gorbachev, 42, 57–58, 71, 128; and coups, 34–35, 47, 71, 166–67, 171, 219; election of, 45–46, 62, 71, 176, 219; government of, 1–3, 58, 102, 119, 123, 124, 128, 134–36, 140–42, 157, 218; leadership of, 143, 158, 162–63, 174–76, 178–79, 181–82, 219–20; and loans for aid, 136; meetings with Clinton, 151–52, 155–57, 168, 177; meetings with Nixon, 41, 140–41, 145–46, 169, 172–75, 183; Nixon's support of, 5, 60, 68, 70,